DECENTRALISED GOVERNMENT AND NGOs

About the Editor

D. Rajasekhar is a development economist based at the Institute for Social and Economic Change, Bangalore. He has published seven books and numerous articles in Indian and international journals on rural credit, NGO savings and credit programmes, interface between 'decentralised' government and NGOs, interface between government and NGOs, agrarian change and transformation, irrigation and rural development. He is currently heading a project on Poverty Alleviation Strategies of NGOs, and working on the impact of micro-finance programmes on poverty and gender equality.

DECENTRALISED GOVERNMENT AND NGOs

ISSUES, STRATEGIES AND WAYS FORWARD

Edited by
D. RAJASEKHAR

CONCEPT PUBLISHING COMPANY, NEW DELHI-110059

ISBN 81-7022-750-X

First Published 1999

Published and Printed by
Ashok Kumar Mittal
Concept Publishing Company
A/15-16, Commercial Block, Mohan Garden
New Delhi 110059 (India)

Phones: 5648039, 5649024
Fax: 091-(11)-5648053

ACKNOWLEDGEMENTS

Ever since 73rd Constitutional Amendment was brought in, Mr. M.K. Bhat, Dr. Neil Webster and myself have been involved in advocating an interface between Panchayat Raj Institutions and NGOs for sustainable people-centered rural development. As a part of these efforts, we have organised several workshops at the Institute for Social and Economic Change, Bangalore, and brought academicians, government officials, donor agencies and NGO activists together to discuss the potentials of the interface, and carry forward the debate and discussions.

One such workshop was organised during January 1997 at the Institute for Social and Economic Change, Bangalore, in collaboration with NOVIB's Consultancy Office, BCO. I thank NOVIB for providing financial support to hold the workshop and for publishing the papers presented in the workshop.

Dr. Neil Webster contributed enormously for the workshop as well as to the publication. He helped me in the selection of the papers and gave comments on the framework of the introduction. I sincerely thank him for his help and support.

Dr. P.V. Shenoi, Director, ISEC, has been a great source of support and encouragement. My heartfelt thanks to him.

Mr. V.S. Parthasarathy extended great support and help in editing the papers. He ensured that papers are well edited, mistakes identified and rectified, and helped me in filling the gaps in the papers. If the number of mistakes are less, it is largely because of him. I place on record my sincere thanks to him.

Ms. M. Shanthi has taken the entire responsibility of word processing. I thank her for her unstinted support and cooperation.

D. RAJASEKHAR

INTRODUCTION

Panchayat Raj Institutions (PRIs) were introduced in India during the 1950s to enable the rural masses to participate in micro-planning and implementation of development projects. The studies on PRIs in several states reveal that the participation of the disadvantaged groups of women and people belonging to Dalit and Adivasi communities in micro-planning was much below the expectations. As a result, the PRIs could not become people-centred, and pro-poor. Politicisation of Panchayats, dominant role played by the vested interests in rural areas, corruption, inadequate devolution of powers and responsibilities to Panchayats, frequent interference into the Panchayat Raj system by the government and officials, irregular elections to Panchayat Raj bodies, etc., were all responsible for this state of affair.

Although PRIs were created in several Indian states, the pre-requisites (Smith 1996) for sustaining the local governance and democracy, and thereby enabling people-centred rural development, were, by and large, absent. An important pre-requisite was an active civil society. Non-governmental organisations (NGOs), as a part of the civil society, were expected (by the aid agencies and government) to play an important role in sustaining the local democracy.

In the past, NGOs were always suspicious of the ability of the PRIs to engage in pro-poor rural development activities. Their view has been that PRIs are usually dominated by vested interests at the village level and that there is a great deal of corruption, a strong pro-rich bias, excessive bureaucratic interference, and party political manipulation. Corruption and bureaucratisation of PRIs have provided very limited scope for the effective participation of the people. Further, any attempt by the NGOs to influence their target group to participate in PRIs would have resulted in a direct confrontation with the village vested interests, which traditionally dominated the PRIs. Party based elections to

PRIs meant that there was less scope for the target group of NGOs to contest and participate in these institutions. For these reasons, the participation of the target group of NGOs in PRIs has always been insignificant in the past.

Considerable devolution of powers to PRIs and reservation of a significant proportion of seats to the disadvantaged groups (women and Dalits) of the population envisaged in the 73rd Constitutional Amendment in 1993 provided an opportunity to the NGOs to closely associate with the PRIs. As the NGOs seek to work for the betterment of the disadvantaged groups which have constitutionally been provided considerable powers and resources through PRIs, there is now scope for these two different actors in rural development to come together in the area of poverty alleviation and in influencing the policies of the government in favour of the poor. Further, the policy that elections to Gram Panchayats are to be held on non-party lines benefits the NGOs interested in enabling their target group to have active engagement with the PRIs.

These factors have contributed to a resurgence of interest[1] in PRIs in NGO circles and have provided an opportunity to NGOs to ensure that PRIs undertake pro-poor developmental activities. Before the elections to Gram Panchayats in four southern states in recent years, the NGOs and their networks in these states not only discussed these elections but also published useful pamphlets on PRIs, their constitution and the opportunities that they provide. They also emphasised the importance of education to voters regarding the type of persons to be elected to PRIs, etc. Some NGOs have encouraged their target group members to participate in the elections for PRIs either as voters or as candidates. NGOs have also played an important role in enabling the target group members to work out strategic alliances and in providing training inputs towards building capacity of the elected members.

While there was interest among certain sections of the NGO sector regarding potential collaboration with the PRIs, there was absence of discussion, and coherent strategy or general agreement on a wide range of issues concerning the relationship between the target group and the PRIs. Some of the more important questions conspicuous for their omission from NGOs' discussions and considerations include: how can better relations between the target group of NGOs and PRIs be brought about? how can cooperation between NGOs regarding collaboration with PRIs be achieved? how would NGOs look at the changing nature and functions of decentralised government? and how do the NGOs and their target group like to make PRIs responsive and responsible for people's needs and grassroots planning and development?

In order to explore some of these issues, a two-day workshop on 'Where are We Now? NGOs and Decentralised Government' was jointly organised by the Institute for Social and Economic Change (ISEC) and NOVIB (DSI) at ISEC, during January, 1997. The ten papers included in this volume are the revised versions of those presented in this workshop[2].

This volume contains eleven papers; six papers written by academics, and the remaining by leaders of five NGOs in Andhra Pradesh, Karnataka and Tamil Nadu. The first paper is an introductory article, while the latter three fall into the category of conceptual papers. The papers by Hansen and Suvarchala are fieldwork based accounts on the impact of interface between Gram Panchayats and the target group of NGOs. The last five papers by NGO leaders document and analyse the strategies adopted by them before, during, and after the elections to Gram Panchayats[3].

The paper by Rajasekhar discusses the context of interface between NGOs and Gram Panchayats. It also discusses the issues, strategies and ways forward by culling out evidence mainly from the papers included in the volume. It also provides a detailed discussion on strategies adopted and difficulties faced by the NGOs, before, during and after the election to Gram Panchayats. This discussion would be useful for those who want to strengthen the interface between NGOs and Gram Panchayats.

The paper by Webster provides the conceptual background to the interface between NGOs and PRIs. This paper, which is an extension to the earlier paper on the subject (Webster 1995), is concerned with three issues; the politics of (re) connecting the local with the state, identification of the poor (i.e., those towards whom NGOs should be directing their work), and who constitute the local in the name of the poor. Webster argues that as the NGOs depend on funding and patronage of the state and donors, they remain more accountable to them; and their development programmes are influenced by the policies of state and donors which visualise only service delivery role for NGOs. He argues that the NGOs must resist the tendencies of having their role defined in this way. Instead, the NGOs need to "take up the task of bringing the local into the arena of high politics where decisions are made, policies are selected, and programmes designed". This is in addition to their role in poverty alleviation. Webster suggests that there is need for a multi-dimensional concept of poverty when thinking about poverty, and for the utilisation of both quantitative and qualitative methodologies when seeking to explore poverty. Third issue that Webster raises is that with so much assistance flowing for local development, there is need for greater clarity on what is local and who constitute the local in the name of the poor.

Aziz, in his paper, notes that two problems are common to most of the Gram Panchayats. First, the members of Gram Panchayats are not able to mobilise the required resources by way of imposing and collecting taxes, and other avenues such as voluntary contributions. Secondly, Gram Panchayat members hardly participate in planning and governance process due to lack of resources (which act as disincentive to members' participation), skills (among Panchayat members in planning and implementation of government programmes), and literacy and education (especially among members belonging to weaker sections). In this context, Aziz notes that the NGOs need to take up the capacity building role since most of the training programmes initiated by the government are not resulting in continuous cumulation of knowledge among Panchayat members. The NGOs would be in a position to provide sustainable training to Panchayat members in the planning and implementation of government programmes.

The paper by Bhat traces the evolution of NGOs since their inception and the position in which they are now. He argues that in the context of adverse impact on the livelihood of the people due to liberalisation policies pursued by the government and privatisation of development, the NGOs face the dual task of collaborating (critically) with the state and at the same time fighting its anti-people, anti-poor and anti-marginalised policies. Such a dual task cannot be discharged effectively unless the NGOs have autonomy based on self-reliance capabilities. Interface between Gram Panchayats and target group of NGOs would contribute to the process of making the development programmes initiated by NGOs sustainable.

The paper by Hansen examines the role of NGOs in facilitating the linkages between their target group and the Gram Panchayats, and the extent to which the NGOs have helped the weaker sections to gain more power within the structure of society. The paper analyses the different approaches that three NGOs from Karnataka have adopted in enabling their target group to participate in the PRIs. She also compares the performance of target group members of NGOs, elected to Gram Panchayats from those villages where NGOs are not working. The main conclusion of Hansen is that the approach followed by NGOs has played an important role in determining the quality of interface between the target group of NGOs and Gram Panchayats. That the NGOs have made a difference is evident from the finding that the participation of members in the control villages is far from satisfactory. They are all name-sake members for their male relatives, do not have any knowledge of the functioning of Gram Panchayat, and do not even attend the meetings, leave alone their participation in the planning and implementation of development programmes.

The paper by Suvarchala analyses the impact of interface between NGOs and decentralised Government on the participation of members at the grassroots level based on data from three Gram Panchayats located in the project area of Young India Project (YIP) in Andhra Pradesh; in all these Panchayats, the YIP union members are in a majority. YIP adopted a three pronged strategy as far as enabling the members of its target group to participate in Gram Panchayats: providing awareness to all the members, independence to village level organisations in selecting the candidates, and in enabling the members to have strategic alliances. The evidence shows that the YIP target group members, especially women, won a large proportion of Gram Panchayat positions in the project area. The profile of elected members shows that many of them who entered the Gram Panchayats for the first time, belonged to the marginalised groups and were illiterate. YIP provided training to them and enabled thc people's organisation to arrive at guidelines for their functioning. Suvarchala argues that while YIP could successfully utilise the policy of reservations in enabling many of its target group members to enter the Gram Panchayats, mere occupation and control of political positions have not resulted in their active and effective participation and exercising of decision-making powers.

Five NGO leaders presented their experiencas with regard to interface with PRIs. These NGOs are Praxis, Young India Project (YIP), Sanghamitra Service Society, SHARE and ROAD. While two NGOs each are located in Andhra Pradesh and Tamil Nadu, one of them is located in Karnataka. These NGOs have undertaken several activities relating to savings and credit, watersheds, mobilisation of the poor, etc. But, the prime concern is to enable the members to have overall empowerment including political. Hence, they consciously tried to facilitate the participation of the target group in the Panchayats. Beginning with a brief background information on the NGOs, each of thc papers discusses the ways in which the interface with PRIs would become important for these organisations to realise the main objective. The papers then go into the details of the strategies adopted in facilitating the linkages with the PRIs before, during, and after the elections to Gram Panchayats.

The papers by NGO leaders show that it is important for them to facilitate their target group to contest in the election to Gram Panchayats. This implies that with the 73rd Amendment to the Constitution of India providing reservations to disadvantaged groups in PRIs and elections to Gram Panchayats on the basis of non-party political symbols, NGOs have greater optimism and confidence in enabling their target group to interact with PRIs, and thereby contributing to people-centred rural development and in sustaining local democracy.

The papers also outline a variety of strategies resorted to enable the target group of NGOs to contest and win in the elections. In addition to the utility that these strategies would have in enabling the other NGOs to have effective interface with the PRIs, they also raise a range of issues relating to local government institutions, legitimacy of NGOs in democratising the society and the role of foreign funding in this regard, etc.

The experience of the NGOs after the elections to Gram Panchayats suggests that the target groups of NGOs are making some efforts to energise Gram Sabhas, make the elected leaders accountable to the people. The experience also shows that the 'room for manoeuvre' for the elected representatives is limited because of lack of funds in Gram Panchayats, party politics, dominant role played by the vested interests, government's programmes and policies, etc.

NOTES

1. A book (Rajasekhar, Bhat and Webster 1995 and a few articles (Dubey 1996; Behar 1998) on the subject have been published.
2. Three papers presented in the workshop are not included in the volume. The paper by Hansen is specifically written for the volume.
3. These strategies are elaborated in Rajasekhar's article in this volume.

REFERENCES

Behar, Amitabh (1998). Revitalising Panchayats: Role of NGOs. *Economic and Political Weekly*, XXXIII (16).

Dubey, Ajay (1996). Strengthening Rural Local Self Government (Panchayat Raj) Institutions: Strategies for NGOs. *Journal of Rural Reconstruction*, 29 (1).

Rajasekhar. D., M.K. Bhat and Neil Webster (eds.) (1995). *People Centred Rural Development· NGDOs and Decentralised Government*. Bangalore: ISEC, CDR, BCO and NOVIB.

Smith, B.C. (1996). Sustainable Local Democracy. *Public Administration and Development*, 16: 163-78.

Webster, Neil (1995). A Conceptual Approach to NGDOs and Panchayat Raj in Rural Development. In D. Rajasekhar *et al.* (1995).

CONTENTS

1

THE INTERFACE BETWEEN GRAM PANCHAYATS AND NGOs: ISSUES, STRATEGIES AND WAYS FORWARD

D. RAJASEKHAR

INTRODUCTION

The rural poor, consisting of landless, small and marginal farmers, face the problems of assetlessness, lack of access to credit, inability to avail the government's anti-poverty programmes, unemployment, poverty, and, are unable to meet the basic needs such as housing, health, education, drinking water, sanitation, etc. These problems are particularly severe in the case of the disadvantaged groups of women, Dalits and Adivasis. To address these problems, large quantum of resources are being expended at the local level by a number of institutions since independence. At various levels of government (Central, state, district and lower), a large number of schemes and programmes[1] have been initiated and considerable amount of investment is being made on various developmental activities. While line ministries/departments are undertaking agricultural and rural development programmes, the formal rural credit delivery system[2] provides finance (credit and subsidies) for these programmes.

However, the strategies of development ranging from individual to community development schemes have failed to take benefits of development to the poor, and to contain the vested interests who oppress and exploit the poor[3], and appropriate the maximum benefits of the government sponsored (and managed) development programmes. It is often felt that the rural development programmes characterise goal confusion, mis-targeting and cuts in subsidies. The problem of leakages, preempting the benefits meant for the poor by the non-poor, is another major hurdle. The larger masses, weak and poor sections of the society are, therefore, subjected to only *theoretical empowerment*[4].

Thus, half-a-century of development efforts initiated largely by the state have not reduced poverty substantially. The problems of hunger, malnutrition, unemployment, gender inequality, illiteracy, etc., continue to persist, though the intensity of these problems seems to have come down in the recent past. One of the important contributing factors for the failure of rural development programmes was the absence of involvement of the people for whom the programmes were meant. The need for micro-level institutional arrangement to involve the people in formulation, implementation and monitoring of the programmes is, therefore, stressed in several quarters.

In fact, this need was felt soon after the independence, and the Panchayat Raj system, based on the recommendations of the Balvantrai Committee, was introduced to create 'a set of institutional frameworks' to make the participation of rural masses more meaningful and effective. The studies on the experience of Panchayat Raj system in several states, however, reveal that the participation of the rural masses consisting largely of disadvantaged groups of women and people belonging to Dalit and Adivasi communities in micro-planning was minimal. This was because of the politicisation of Panchayats, dominant role played by the vested interests in rural areas[5], corruption, inadequate devolution of powers and responsibilities to Panchayats, frequent interference into Panchayat Raj system by the government and its officials, irregular elections to Panchayat Raj bodies, etc. (Mathew 1994). As a result, the decentralised structure in the form of a 'four pillar state', resting on the foundations of a four-fold sharing of power between the village, the district, state and the centre, and bringing about a people-centered rural development remained more in the realm of an idea than in the practice.

Following the report of the Asoka Mehta Committee, and the experiences of the states of West Bengal[6] and Karnataka[7] in decentralised governance, the discussion on how to secure people's participation in the development process through Panchayat Raj institutions (PRIs) and devolution of powers continued. The discussion was also influenced by the world-wide debate on the need to involve people in their own development. The aid agencies, multilateral and bilateral, have also stressed the need to revitalise the Panchayats to secure people's participation in the development process. Subsequently, the Indian government brought in the 73rd Constitutional Amendment in 1993. The Amendment sought to bring a new political system in rural areas by giving priority to decentralisation, people's participation and democracy at the local level. The Amendment adopted a three-tier model with democratically elected governments at the village, Taluk or Mandal and district level. The Gram Sabha (people's assembly) consisting of all voters in a Gram Panchayat area is to be convened at least twice a year to incorporate people's views into planning and implementation.

The Amendment incorporated the following mandatory rules to secure people's participation in PRIs: (i) elections to PRIs are to be held regularly, and at the village level they should be held on non-party lines; (ii) seats are to be reserved for women and persons belonging to SC/ST categories in PRIs at different levels; (iii) mandatory elections to PRIs, after completing their five-year term; (iv) mandatory constitution of a Finance Commission once in five years to review the finances and to recommend the size of funds to be allocated to the Panchayats and also the principles and the basis on which taxes should be collected in Panchayat areas; (v) PRIs are made responsible to implement the government schemes and programmes aimed at economic development and social justice in rural areas; and (vi) the responsibility of collecting taxes is placed with the Panchayats.

The amendment was hailed as an important landmark for its radical approach towards decentralisation, devolution of power and in ensuring the participation of the marginalised sections. The available studies, though not many, suggest that while the marginalised groups have entered the PRIs, their effective participation in these bodies is yet to be achieved. First, the political parties do not seem to be serious about the decentralisation and devolution of power. A comparative study on the track record of several national and regional political parties reveals that "while almost all the national and regional parties have promised to make Panchayats strong and viable if they are voted to power, none of them has gone beyond promising more than what they did in their manifestos... At the same time, their track record reveals that except the Left parties, none of them is serious about decentralisation" (Pal 1998b: 631). The provision for reservation of 30 per cent of the seats at all levels of the PRIs for women is perceived as a crucial step for their empowerment. But, the experiences of training camps for women Panchayat members reveal that there is little awareness among women about the possibilities that the new reservation policy would open up for the articulation of their rights (Pal 1998a). Similarly, a study of three villages in Meerut district in Uttar Pradesh cautions that without female literacy, independent voting rights and change in status of women in the family and society, women will continue to act as name-sake representatives of the male members of their households (Pai 1998).

Thus, the studies suggest that mere constitutional changes do not bring radical improvement in decentralisation and people's participation. In this context, the distinction between administrative and political decentralisation (Hansen in this volume) becomes relevant. In administrative decentralisation, certain changes (initiated from outside or from inside) would lead to an improvement in the implementation of development projects. Political aspects remain secondary concern under this approach. On the other hand, political decentralisation involves the transfer of decision-making authority to previously under-represented or marginal groups. While administrative decentralisation approach claims that mere structural changes will lead to a higher degree of development, the political approach argues that mobilisation of people and devolution of power are necessary to obtain real decentralisation.

Viewed from this angle, the 73rd Constitutional Amendment which sought to ensure the participation of women and marginalised groups through reservations can be questioned on the grounds that reservations cannot break the traditional patterns of socio-economic and political structures in the countryside and bring awareness and power to the people belonging to the marginalised groups overnight (Hansen, in this volume). There must be enabling conditions such as people's organisations, efforts aimed at improving literacy and functional skills, and improving the confidence of women and marginalised groups, etc. There is, therefore, a need to look at the other actors who can provide such enabling conditions so that decentralisation, devolution of powers and participation of the marginalised groups, provided in the Amendment, can be utilised to secure people-centered rural development. Now, it is widely believed that Non-Governmental Organisations (NGOs), which have come up on a large scale in several parts of India, have the potential to create such conditions to enable the people[8] to participate effectively in the local government.

NON-GOVERNMENTAL ORGANISATIONS IN INDIA

NGOs are those organisations which possess four distinct characteristics: *voluntary formation, working towards development, working with non-self serving aims and relative independence.* NGOs are voluntarily formed in the sense that (ideally speaking) there is no compulsion from government or others which leads to their formation. There is also a notion of voluntarism in the fact that the staff, especially at the leadership levels, work at salaries below what they can draw in the government or the private sector. This, however, may not apply to funding agencies or to professional NGOs. They are development oriented in the sense that they are concerned with improving the condition and position of oppressed sections of society, as opposed to other goals like entertainment, promotion of religion, etc. Finally, they are relatively, but not completely, independent from the government in the sense that their policies are determined by their Board of Directors or Trustees who need not be drawn from the government. However, the NGOs have to work within the parameters of government legislations and policies formulated for NGOs (Murthy 1998).

Types and function of NGOs

NGOs can be divided into four broad categories; operational or grassroots NGOs, support NGOs, network NGOs and funding NGOs. The functions of each type of NGOs are explained below.

Operational or Grassroots NGOs directly work with the oppressed sections of society. Some of the grassroots NGOs are big, while some are small[9]. Depending on who has founded, the grassroots NGOs can be divided into three types: private NGOs (formed by an individual or group of individuals), GONGOs (formed by the Government) and DONGOs (initiated by the Donor agencies). Based on the approach and orientation of grassroots NGOs, which differ, the following distinction can be made: (i) 'charity and welfare NGOs' focus on providing charity and welfare to the poor; (ii) 'development NGOs' focus on implementation of concrete development activities; (iii) 'social action groups' focus on mobilising marginalised sections around specific issues which challenge the distribution of power and resources in society; and (iv) 'empowerment NGOs' combine development activities with issue based struggles.

The approaches and activities followed by the first-two types of NGOs, which are related to the strengthening of delivery system, are non-controversial and do not lead to clash of interests in the countryside. Hence, the government too extends full support to NGOs working in these areas. Activities undertaken by the last two types of NGOs are basically related to the strengthening of 'recipient system', and the approach to development is political. Hence, their activities are often politicised. The relief oriented NGOs are on the decline, and not much of funding support is extended to them, as it is felt that their strategy is not based on building the capacity of the people, and making the programmes sustainable. It is to be, however, noted that the last two types of NGOs may also, at times, take up relief and rehabilitation activities depending on the circumstances.

Support NGOs provide services that would strengthen the capacities of grassroots NGOs, PRIs, cooperatives and others to function more effectively. Some do not engage in grassroots action while others do have field projects, but grassroots action is not their primary task. Some of the support NGOs render support in specific thematic areas such as health, education and environment, while others provide support in generic issues such as perspectives, leadership, human resources development, operations management and organisation development. The former support organisations can be called as thematic specific support organisations while the latter can be called as generic support organisations (Murthy 1998).

Umbrella or Network NGOs are formal associations or informal groups of grassroots and/or support NGOs which meet periodically on particular concerns. They provide a forum to share micro-level experiences, and carry out joint development endeavours and lobbying and advocacy. The participation of network NGOs in lobbying and advocacy is, however, a recent phenomenon.

Funding NGOs mainly provide funding to grassroots NGOs, support NGOs or people's organisations. Most funding NGOs in India generate a major part of their resources from foreign sources though there is an effort by some to raise funds from within India. In addition, Northern NGOs like Netherlands International Development Cooperation (NOVIB), Action Aid, Oxfam, etc., with headquarters in the developed western countries, mobilise resources from both the public and governments in their respective countries to help grassroots NGOs in their efforts to initiate and implement pro-poor rural development activities. Northern NGOs do have field officers here. Some bilateral agencies like German Development Corporation (GTZ/SHF), etc., do provide funding support to NGOs; but, these cannot be called as NGOs.

Evolution of NGO movement in India

The development perspective of NGOs shifted from the ideology of charity and service delivery in the early 1970s to conscientization, mobilisation of the marginalised sections, integrated development and empowerment[10]. Now-a-days many NGOs state that they are working on sustainable development. This is, however, does not mean that all the NGOs belong to the same category. Over the wide-spectrum of NGOs in India, one can find various types of NGOs belonging to several perspectives explained above (Bhat, in this volume).

There is also a shift in the role of NGOs. In the early 1970s, NGOs were directly implementing charity and welfare programmes. Subsequently, the NGOs started emphasising what was called 'intervention strategy' in which the NGO's role was temporary. In 1980s, the NGOs started talking in terms of facilitator role. Now-a-days, the NGOs are supposed to assume only support role.

A detailed discussion on the evolution of NGO movement (Rajasekhar 1998c) suggests that the above changes in the development perspective of NGOs were influenced by (i) the contemporary thinking and ideology on development; (ii) the existing government programmes, and the role foreseen for NGOs in the implementation of these programmes; and (iii) aid philosophy of the donor agencies and their development priorities.

INTERFACE BETWEEN GRAM PANCHAYATS AND NGOs

It is widely believed (and accepted) that NGOs have several advantages[11]. First, NGOs tend to be more actor oriented because they represent local interests[12]. Second, NGOs exhibit a high degree of flexibility in their functioning, methods and practices because they tend to be local and small[13]. Third, NGO development programmes tend to be innovative and emphasise on participatory approaches. Fourth, NGO development work tends to be more focused as it is their principal goal[14]. Fifth, NGO development programmes enjoy independence; their governing boards are autonomous; and their development activities are primarily meant for the target group[15]. Sixth, NGO development programmes tend to be effective in reaching the poor and poverty alleviation[16]. Seventh, compared to government agencies, NGOs have several advantages[17]. Eighth, NGOs have potential to play an important role in influencing the state policies by advocacy and lobbying through their networks.

These potential advantages contributed to the increasing popularity of the NGOs among the government and external aid agencies. As a result, the number of NGOs increased rapidly in recent years[18] Edwards and Hulme (1995 and 1996) argue that the growing number of NGOs is because of their increasing popularity with governments and official aid agencies, which is itself a response to recent developments in economic and political thinking. In recent years, the development policy of aid agencies such as the World Bank, and aid transfers from them, have come to be dominated by what is referred to as 'New Policy Agenda', which gives a prominent role to the NGOs in poverty alleviation, social welfare, and the development of civil society (Robinson 1993). The Agenda has two elements: economic and political.

The New Economic Policy Agenda, followed in India since 1991, sees the markets and private sector as more efficient in producing goods and services and in achieving rapid economic growth. This philosophy seems to be increasingly extended to social services for the poor, with NGOs taking over this role from the government. NGOs are seen as cost effective and efficient service providers, and successful in reaching those poor who may *not* be reached by the market process or the state (Bhat 1995: 48-99).

The political dimension of the Agenda sees that democratisation of the society is an important pre-requisite[19] for the success of the Agenda's economic dimension (Moore 1993). And, NGOs are seen as an "integral component of a thriving civil society[20] and an essential counterweight to state power, opening up channels of communication and participation, providing training grounds for activists, and promoting pluralism" (Edwards and Hulme 1996: 962).

Because of these factors, the last ten years witnessed improved credibility and legitimacy for NGOs. Compared to earlier decades, NGOs now have better space to collaborate with the government and influence the policy at different levels. The government has been discussing with the prominent NGO leaders about the ways and means by which collaboration between the government and NGOs could be improved. Some prominent NGO leaders found a place in key decision-making bodies, committees, etc. Several ministries and departments in the Central government and several state governments are actively seeking the views of NGOs in the policy formulation and programmes implementation. Notwithstanding the charges of corruption and lack of accountability and public transparency on some of the NGOs, there is considerable credibility and legitimacy for the NGOs today.

With large number of NGOs, and increased funding, the NGOs are able to create vast social infrastructure. Even if we assume that each of the NGO, which is active in rural development, is working in 10 villages, the NGOs together would be covering half-of-the villages in India. Even if we assume that each of the NGO has five trained workers, the number of qualified persons engaged in rural development would be large. All the NGOs have formed people's organisations at the village level, provided education and training to the people in various issues, and all of them work with the groups traditionally marginalised such as women, Dalits and Adivasis.

This social infrastructure created by NGOs provides ample opportunities as far as enabling the poor and marginalised groups to enter into Gram Panchayats, in improving their capacity as Gram Panchayat members and in making Gram Panchayats pro-poor and people-centered (Bhat, in this volume). It may be mentioned here that as a result of the 73rd Constitutional Amendment, about 34 lakhs of elected representatives of Panchayats at all levels have been in position as members and chairpersons (Pal 1998b). This represents the broadest base at the grassroots in the world. About half-of-these persons belong to the marginalised groups of women, SCs and STs, and many of them would have entered into the Panchayats for the first time. There is urgent need to build the capacity of these persons so that they can effectively participate in the Panchayats.

What are the areas in which NGOs need to intervene? Aziz, based on years of research work on Gram Panchayats, identified three levels at which NGOs can play a role in revitalising Gram Panchayats: (i) motivate people, especially those belonging to weaker sections, to participate in the elections (both as voters and candidates) in view of the intimidating role played by the vested interests; (ii) motivate people to participate in the planning and implementation process by regularly attending Gram sabha meetings; and (iii) play a constructive role in augmenting Panchayat resources by enabling Panchayat members to depend more on local resources, and by urging the people in the Panchayat area to contribute resources. At the second level, the NGOs need to provide information (on Panchayat governance and planning, role, rights and privileges of Panchayat members, etc.) and inputs on attitudinal changes, for example, with regard to reservations for the weaker sections. At the third level, the NGOs need to provide inputs to Panchayat members in planning and implementation of development programmes. They also need to build the capacity of local bureaucracy by providing them information on number of the poor, inventory of amenities, village level problems, etc.

The task of capacity building of these persons cannot be effectively undertaken by the government agencies. It is impossible for the government to reach 34 lakhs of elected representatives in the country, and even if the government aims to provide capacity building inputs to those who have been elected on reserved seats, the task is enormous. It is in this context that the social infrastructure created by the NGOs would become relevant. The NGOs have comparative advantages as far as reaching this number as they are known in the area, and also in providing the capacity building inputs to the elected members because NGOs not only speak the local language but also have rapport with the people.

When it comes to interface between Panchayats and the target group of NGOs, there are questions on what should be the nature of interface. These questions become relevant in the context of change in the perspective of NGOs largely due to the influence of policies of the state and aid agencies, increased funding and legitimacy for the NGO work. They also become relevant in the context of criticisms on NGOs regarding their transparency, accountability, etc.

There is need for the interface to go beyond the capacity building of the elected representatives. The NGOs need to facilitate those conditions which enable the marginalised groups to enter into Gram Panchayats, and sustain the process of people-centered rural development. This calls for a change in the role of NGOs from mere service delivery to connecting the local with macro policies.

It is argued that the role of NGOs should not be confined to the mere service delivery. The evidence on performance of NGOs in service delivery is mixed. While the quality of service delivery tends to be good[21], questions are raised on the cost effectiveness of service delivery (Riddel and Robinson 1992), targeting of the inputs[22], sustainable service provision and poverty reduction[23]. 'Spatial limitation' (Webster 1995b: 427) also does not enable the NGOs to provide services in a sustainable manner. Service provision by NGOs also makes the people more dependent on NGOs and influences them to turn away from the government with which they have more legitimate relationship. This suggests that there are limitations to NGOs in so far as provision of services and that the state still has (would have) considerable role to play in service delivery, and that NGOs cannot replace the state in this important function. Increased role for NGOs in service provision can make the state perpetually inefficient in discharging its duties to its citizens, and can relieve the state from pressures of providing efficient services. This, in turn, adversely affects those poor who are not covered by the NGOs within (and also outside) their project areas.

While the service provision by NGOs may be needed in certain regions, for certain groups and at specific points of time, mere service provision may not become sustainable, it may become palliative and become barrier to important structural changes in the ownership of land and other capital assets. The viable strategy for NGOs would, therefore, be to facilitate those mechanisms through which the people (that they work with) would demand the government to deliver more goods and services, and help them put pressure on the state to become a better developer. For this, lobbying and advocacy through networks become important.

Individual NGOs are rarely in a position to influence policy at state level in India — Federal or Union. In addition, rarely do they seek to influence policy, because, as noted earlier, their existence and tolerance by the state is based upon a non-controversial, apolitical involvement in development. Furthermore, NGOs rarely cooperate and liaise with one another, tending instead to view each other as competitors for donor funding, state tolerance, and on occasions, local influence and space (Rajasekhar and Nair 1995). Consequently, they fail to emerge as genuine macro actors, at regional or at national levels, seeking to represent their members' interests in the political process of governance and more general development (Webster 1995a).

In this context, the role visualised for NGOs in developing interface with decentralised government is that in addition to facilitating the formation of people's organisations for making efforts to alleviate poverty, the NGOs need to connect local with the state (Webster, in this volume) through critically collaborating with local development agencies including line departments and decentralised government. With regard to decentralised government, the NGOs need to enable the target group to participate in the political process, enable them to take part in Gram Panchayats in planning and implementation of development programmes, and represent the interests of the poor at higher levels of decision-making through lobbying and advocacy.

Making a similar point, Bhat argues that "the sustainability of the grassroots level, people-centered, participatory and self-managed development processes will ultimately depend on the capability of the people in local resource mobilisation and influencing policy processes. Mere assertion of rights through social mobilisation and democratic pressure will not satisfy their basic and development needs. Entering the governance at the local level and bringing in a qualitative change in the local bodies in favour of the poor and marginalised could integrate equity principle and sustainability factor into micro development processes. This, in turn, could strengthen the bottom-up development processes with its impact on the so-called mainstream development. The vast social infrastructure of the poor and marginalised, the women, the Dalits, the Adivasis, the agricultural labourers, etc., promoted by the NGOs all over the country exhibits such potential and possibilities explained above. However, transforming them into reality depends very much on the political initiative of the people which, in turn, depends on the perspectives with which NGOs organise them". This is further supported by Hansen's argument that it is the approach of the NGOs which become important as far as effective interface between NGOs and Gram Panchayats is concerned. It is in this context that we need to examine the perspectives of the NGOs on interface with PRIs.

Perspective of NGOs on interface with PRIs

NGOs seem to be having several perspectives on the need for interface with PRIs. The first perspective is that interface with Gram Panchayat is needed to bring political empowerment. For instance, Praxis notes that "development has to be understood in political terms. It is only the political power that determines the shape of the destiny of the people. To bring about development from the point of view of the poor, they need to be in the mainstream of politics, and control political power. This calls for political empowerment of the poor". Similar views have been presented by the other organisations. According to ROAD, politically empowered women are in a better position to have command over resources and other structures prevailing in the society. Wherever possible, women, therefore, need to enter into the positions of decision-making.

The second perspective is that interface with PRIs is needed to carry out the struggles. For instance, YIP believes that social transformation of Bourgeois Democracy, which, in India, is really an elected oligarchy (Government of the rich), cannot come about except through the struggles of the classes and gender which have been marginalised economically, socially and politically by the richer classes. YIP, therefore, accepted the strategy of a permanent struggle against capitalism to transform it to socialism, and the YIP also has come to believe that, in this struggle, the rural poor masses are the main force of transformation. The support has been provided in the form of ideological inputs, organisational inputs and finally, coordination and guidance of the struggles taken up by the masses. Hence, YIP is convinced that Panchayat elections should become a major issue for struggle by the rural poor using reservations to their advantage.

The third perspective is that interface with the PRIs helps in bringing about right political culture among the marginalised groups such as Dalits. For instance, Praxis is working among Dalits, and leaders elected from among Dalits are being coopted into the mainstream political process. Hence, the organisation gives considerable importance to building skills and capacity of Dalits. When it comes to elections to Gram Panchayats and the poor, one has to recognise that there are several tasks such as providing political education to the exploited class. There is need to understand the new kind of politics which departs from the hitherto existing political culture and values.

Fourth, interface with PRIs is helpful in developing political leadership among the marginalised groups. At the present level of development, the Dalits and the poor from the villages are not able to participate and get elected to the state assemblies. The Panchayats are the only government bodies that are within their reach. These elections are seen both as opportunity to capture power at the lower level and also to learn about politics and acquire skills to become politicians in the future.

Fifth, it is also believed that interface with PRIs helps women to participate in decision-making within the community. For instance, SHARE felt it necessary to widen its area of operation (from economic and welfare activities) to encompass issues and matters that will be helpful in the long run to make it possible for women to increase their level of participation in decision making at the community level.

Sixth, interface with PRIs provides an opportunity to enable the poor to access the resources. Praxis thinks that the organisation could work at the Panchayat level both to elect the desirable members and also get elected to the Panchayats. This ensures that the opportunities available at the local government for the development of the poor are utilised to the maximum. Sanghamitra Service Society (hereafter, Sanghamitra) also notes that when it comes to the implementation of the developmental activities and people's participation, the PRIs are not able to properly fulfil their responsibility because of the vested interests. The people, especially the poor, are also not aware of the functioning of the PRIs and they are also not trained in this regard. Social issues like caste, economic status, etc., are contributing to the lack of participation from the people. Sanghamitra believes that if PRIs are strengthened, and the poor are made to involve, then the role of vested interests would gradually weaken and pro-poor development can take place.

Strategies adopted during the pre-election phase

NGOs adopted various strategies before, during and after the elections to Gram Panchayats. These strategies were arrived at after the discussions with the target group members, and/or were learnt in training programmes, workshops, etc. The strategies adopted by NGOs are elaborated below.

* Carrying out campaigns aimed at providing information on the Panchayat elections and New Panchayat Raj Bill. The main aim of the campaign is to make the people aware of the value of their votes and how the votes help them in electing right candidate, etc.
* Sending staff members for training to those institutions or agencies specialised in PRIs to acquire good knowledge about the Act, obtain relevant documents and material, etc. This process helped to prepare a few of the staff members as trainers.

* Organising training programmes for leaders and representatives. The training programmes were conducted by the staff members, who have had prior training, or by experts from outside or by both. In some of the NGO project areas, training was separately organised for women. Realising that the rural poor had never contested Panchayat elections, massive training programmes were organised to make them understand how reservations could be used to their advantage. In the training programmes, people were explained about the history of Panchayat Raj in India, 73rd Constitutional Amendment, the opportunities that the new institutions provide to the poor, planning and campaigning for the Panchayat elections, problems to be faced from local landlords and politicians, how do rigging and other malpractices take place in the elections, etc.
* Training methodology emphasised on street plays, songs and other local popular media. For this, cultural teams were developed. The YIP produced a movie on how to contest in the coming elections and this was shown in all the Panchayats where there were strong groups. In general, class room lectures were kept to the minimum.
* Often, it is questioned that whether NGOs have legitimacy to work for democratisation of society with foreign funding. Hence, some of the NGOs adopted the strategy of training the members through funds received from government agencies such as Council for the Advancement of People's Action and Rural Technology (CAPART).
* One of the organisations conducted evaluation programmes to find out the impact of both the campaigns and training programmes on members.
* Collecting information about Gram Panchayat elections, seat distribution and reserved seats from government offices.
* Independence was given to village level organisations to choose their own candidates for the election, and the NGO staff did not intervene in the process. But, one of the NGOs sought to educate the members of Sanghas on how to select a candidate

based on certain criteria such as sincerity and honesty, education, leadership qualities, capability to stand and win the elections, capacity to deliver goods after the elections. It was also suggested that a member who had comparative advantages should be selected.

Difficulties faced during the pre-election phase

* Although reservations have been provided to enable the disadvantaged groups to contest in the elections, people belonging to these groups did not, on their own, come forward to contest in the elections. At the same time, the vested interests in local areas were trying to field their own followers as proxy candidates in the elections with the sole purpose of controlling the Panchayats and thwarting the very purpose of providing reservations to these groups. The vcry contest of members of the NGO target group in the elections resulted in tensions and conflicts in the village.
* The selection of candidates was not a smooth process. Many wanted to contest in the elections, and members of the village organisations could not come to a consensus. As a result, the target group members either joined hands with the vested interests in the village or worked against the candidate chosen by the group, resulting in a situation where two candidates from one group contested against each other (in the process, both the candidates lost the elections), etc.

Strategies adopted during the phase of elections

* Sanghamitra provided moral support to the candidates. As a majority of the candidates stood for the elections for the first time, there was need to support and instil confidence in them. There was also need to look into the tendencies that force members to withdraw from election process. It organised Sangha meetings before the elections to educate the members regarding prevention of clashes and cross voting.
* YIP adopted an election strategy under which the people's organisation at Mandal level was advised and guided to select

Panchayats to contest where membership was the highest. A strategy was also worked out to select candidates for reserved seats with participation of all the community members of the castes for which the seats were reserved. If there were two seats reserved for SCs, and not all the SC families were members of the union, then a deal was negotiated wherein one candidate was selected from among the non-union families, and another from the union families. The agreement being that the union would vote for the non-union candidate and the non-union members would vote for the union candidate in case of third or a fourth member also deciding to contest with the support of the landed classes. This understanding was arrived at with SC, ST, BC and minority communities.

* There were also strategic alliances with the political parties without subscribing to any party's ideology and getting coopted into it. In some Panchayats, where Congress candidates were strong, the YIP union made an alliance with the Telugu Desam Party (TDP) to get its members elected. In those Panchayats where TDP was strong, alliances were formed with the Congress party.
* The selection of candidates for Ward and Sarpanch seats, and the alliance/understanding to be arrived at, were left to the people's organisations because they best understood the power relations at the local level.

Difficulties faced during the phase of elections

* Despite the best preparations, the rich and powerful people in the villages threatened and prevented the poor to participate in the voting, indulged in rigging, etc. (See, Boxes 8.1 and 8.2). The target group organisation resorted to legal activism in such cases.
* Though the elections were supposed to be held on the basis of non-political party symbols, people behaved and voted on the basis of the party affiliation of the candidates.
* The candidates belonging to the NGO target group canvassed for votes by putting forth only their selflessness and concern

for the community. But, the common persons in the villages voted for those who paid money and who supplied liquor.

* In some cases, even though the women were motivated and prepared to participate in the elections to the PRI, they did not get the wholehearted support from their husbands/parents/families.
* One common observation was that the Returning Officer and his team members allowed themselves to be entertained by influential politicians and this adversely affected the morale of the women contestants. This had also led them to believe that these officials would in some way or the other be taking sides with the party candidate.
* The Ward system is different from the system of constituency. In some cases, though members of Sangha held the required number of votes for winning the election, the candidates chosen by the Sangha lost because of Ward system.

Strategies adopted during the phase of post-elections

* If the participation of the disadvantaged groups in Gram Panchayats is important to make the bodies people-centred, there is a need to provide considerable support to these groups to enable them to participate effectively in Gram Panchayats. Otherwise, the vested interests in rural areas would continue to play a dominant role in the functioning of Gram Panchayats. Realising that most of the Panchayat members did not have previous experience in Panchayat management, training programmes were organised.
* For these training programmes, some of the NGOs invited only those members who belonged to their own target group. On the other hand, some of the NGOs encouraged all the Gram Panchayat members belonging to different castes and communities to participate in the training programme. According to these NGOs, through such programmes, it was possible to win over many more Panchayat members. But, this depended on the number of members to be trained. In the case of YIP, which had thousands of its own target group

members to be trained, the training programmes concentrated only on its own target group members.

* Some of the NGOs prepared manuals on 'how to run a Panchayat?' The topics covered were — what is the role of Gram Panchayat in development, how development funds would be channelled from district to village Panchayat, the decision-making process in a Gram Panchayat and rules and regulations concerning meetings, responsibilities, use of funds, etc. Thus, the training emphasised on the provision of information as well as building the skills of the elected members.
* One or two-day training conducted for Sarpanches and Ward members had failed to produce the desired impact especially in the case of women. Even after training, they allowed their husbands to attend and participate in Gram Panchayat meetings. It is now realised by some NGOs that one day training by itself would not suffice, and that a long term follow-up strategy is also needed to enable SC, ST, BC and women elected under reservation to participate actively in Gram Panchayat meetings and decision-making. Subsequently, it was decided that each Mandal leader-cum-union Secretary must adopt 4 to 5 Gram Panchayats to do follow-up work which would include attending meetings, maintaining minutes and keeping record of developmental funds received by each adopted Gram Panchayat and how they have been utilised.
* Some of the NGOs adopted the strategy of receiving funds from CAPART for the training programmes as this would provide legitimacy.

Difficulties faced during the phase of post-elections

* In most of the Gram Panchayats, the funds for development works are either meagre or non-existent. This provides very limited scope for members of Gram Panchayats to effectively participate in planning and implementation of the activities.
* One problem (in Andhra Pradesh) is that the cheque signing authority was not transferred from the previously appointed

Sarpanches to the newly elected Sarpanches until a year after the elections. Even after the state government passed a G.O. giving the new elected Sarpanches and Group Executive Officer (GEO) cheque signing authority, the Panchayat presidents belonging to upper castes refused to hand over the accounts, the cheque books, and the Panchayat files to the new Sarpanches belonging to the SC, ST, BC communities.

* The powers of Gram Panchayats are constantly usurped by the government and the bureaucracy. An example to this is the introduction of Prajala Vaddaku Palana (PVP) programme in Andhra Pradesh. Under the PVP, a nodal officer was appointed for each Mandal and along with him or her, Mandal officials were required to visit each Gram Panchayat, hold meetings with all the members of the Panchayats inclusive of the elected Sarpanches and Ward members and make a list of works to be undertaken in the Gram Panchayat area under the PVP, with 50 per cent of the cost of the work being contributed by the members of the Gram Panchayat in the form of *shramadan* or free labour. The balance 50 per cent funds being released by the state as PVP funds. This meant that development funds became PVP funds to be channelled not through the PRIs but through the official machinery. This also meant that the powers and responsibilities that had been given to the grassroots elected leaders through the 73rd Amendment were taken back through the PVP. Now, though the Sarpanches have cheque signing authority, there are no funds in the Gram Panchayats for the Sarpanches and GEO to sign the cheque. In addition, there is no point in holding the Panchayat meetings to make decisions on developmental programmes to be taken up within the Gram Panchayats because such decisions are taken not in Gram Panchayat meetings but in PVP meetings.

WAYS FORWARD

The foregoing discussion raises several issues. The discussion on strategies adopted and difficulties faced by NGOs before, and after the elections to Gram Panchayats suggests that the NGOs need to concentrate on the following issues in the future.

Target group approach

NGOs often follow target group approach in the villages where they are working. In other words, they would be working with only a handful of households in the villages. It would be, therefore, difficult for the target group members to win in the elections on their own as they may not command the required majority in the village. Faced with this kind of situation, the NGOs enabled the members of their target group to have strategic alliances with those sections of the village (which are closer to this group in political, social and economic terms) in such a way that both the groups would stand to gain in the elections.

The interface between the NGOs and Gram Panchayats become important because of the powers and responsibilities vested with the latter. The policy of reservations for the disadvantaged groups was meant to pave the way of Gram Panchayats to become pro-poor in their approach and orientation. The disadvantaged groups cannot, however, freely participate in the election process largely because of lack of confidence and lack of money to spend in elections. Some of the NGOs, therefore, provided non-monetary support to the weaker sections to contest in the elections. However, the people belonging to the weaker sections also need money to be spent in the elections. SHARE raises this question. In this context, some important questions that arise are: Can NGOs sustain the provision of support to its target group members? What are the implications of foreign funding in this regard? The NGOs need to realise that it is possible to mobilise resources from the government, as has been done by YIP.

The next issue relating to the target group is that NGOs need to provide voter's education and awareness on PRIs to all the poor in the project area rather than only to their target group. Similarly, they need to build the capacity of all those representatives who were elected on reservation in the project area, rather than only to their target group members.

Local resource mobilisation

In the present context, the resource mobilisation, largely from within the Gram Panchayat area, becomes important. As per the 73rd Amendment, the Gram Panchayats have been empowered to impose certain type of taxes. When it comes to imposing taxes to mobilise the local resources, the members of the Panchayat seem to be having problems such as fear of losing popularity with the voters, limited diversification of activities in the Gram Panchayat area coming in the way of broad-basing the tax structure, the poverty in the area, etc. Another problem could be lack of knowledge among Gram Panchayat members. There is, therefore, need to improve the capacity of the members of Gram Panchayats in this regard. Similarly, Gram Panchayats are required to mobilise free labour and donations, etc., from the public to undertake certain types of development activities for which resources coming from outside may not be sufficient. Experiences with a few Gram Panchayats in Karnataka and Andhra Pradesh show that there is very little happening in this regard. This is because people are not convinced about the ability of the Gram Panchayat to play a pro-poor role. These issues need to be taken up by the NGOs in future.

Meetings of Gram Sabhas

Now it has become mandatory for Gram Panchayats to convene Gram sabhas once in six months to assess the needs of the people. Although the evidence of convening the Gram sabhas in Karnataka does exist, these Gram sabhas do not seem to be serving the purpose. First of all, these meetings normally reflect the views of the president and the members of Gram Panchayats. Secondly, Gram sabhas, if at all they are convened, end up in intense conflict and do not even reach the agenda point. Thirdly, the officials do not seem to be attending the Gram sabha meetings.

Given that Gram Sabhas are to be convened to assess the needs of the members, the importance of active participation of people in Gram sabha cannot be overemphasised. However, the NGOs have a dilemma with regard to making Gram sabhas active and dynamic. This is because of the fact that NGOs work with only a small proportion of the people within the village. A question has been raised as to whether the NGOs need to work with the village as a whole for the limited purpose of enabling an active participation in Gram Sabhas. Bhat argues that the target group of NGOs, if it is educated, enlightened and empowered, can play an important role as an 'effective minority' to energise the Gram sabha. One of the NGOs in Karnataka believes in, and adopts, effective minority strategy. The papers included in this volume suggest that nothing much is happening in this area.

Political *vs* non-political strategies

While suggesting the interface between NGOs and Gram Panchayats, we are making an implicit assumption that they can work together. This, however, may not be realised. This is because the Gram Panchayat members are suspicious of NGOs in some of the villages in Karnataka that we visited. At the same time, some of the NGOs do not think that Gram Panchayats can be pro-poor because of the domination of PRIs by vested interests. The research done by Westergaard (1995) in Bangladesh shows that there are limits to the interface between NGOs and PRIs. According to her, the local vested interests would not allow the weaker sections to capture all the political power through Gram Panchayats at the local level. The NGOs adopted several strategies in this regard.

It can be argued that results are likely to be favourable if the NGOs follow political approach. Hansen's study (in this volume) shows that one of the sample NGOs, which adopted political approach to Gram Panchayat, is far more successful in enabling the marginalised groups to participate in the Gram Panchayats. In this project area, the members elected to Gram Panchayats have obtained experience and skills in analysing and addressing the problems at the village level as Sangha members. With a little training support, they could pick up nuances of Gram Panchayat functioning and their role as Gram Panchayat members. The elected Gram Panchayat members were far more accountable to the Sangha which helped them to get elected.

On the other hand, the participation of women members, from the other two NGOs which adopted different approach in Gram Panchayats,is not that encouraging. In these organisations, the participation of members in Gram Panchayats is not qualitatively different due to lack of strong people's organisations, lack of emphasis to build the skills and capacity of the target group members from the beginning, and short (and one-off) training programmes. The performance of the members also varied on the basis of the period of NGO association with the villages. In the older villages, there were good linkages between elected members and Sangha; in the relatively new villages, elected members were not accountable to Sangha.

But, adoption of political approach to deal with the local vested interests is not something which is liked by the NGOs. While NGOs could adopt non-political approach as short-term strategy, there is need to note that unless the weaker sections bargain for the political space, nothing much may happen in the future. In this context, the strategy adopted by the YIP, Penugonda, is interesting, and valuable lessons could be learnt from this experience (Bedi in this volume).

From the available reports, it is noticed that the role the target group of NGOs played in PRIs varied. Some of the NGOs in Karnataka adopted four strategies, limited engagement, direct employment, indirect political engagement and direct political engagement (Rajasekhar 1995). Whatever may have been the strategies, the target group in the case of a majority of the NGOs did not succeed in having decisive majority in Gram Panchayats. In those Gram Panchayats where the target group of NGOs did not have decisive majority, the local vested interests continued to play a dominant role and did not allow the target group of NGOs to play any effective role. In such cases, as Sivaji's paper shows, the 'room for manoeuvre' is limited.

Even in those Panchayats where the target group members had decisive majority, the participation of members did not significantly improve. The evidence presented by Suvarchala (in this volume) suggests the following: First, although the meetings were convened at short notice and without circulating an agenda, the target group members belonging to YIP did not protest it. Second, despite the fact that the target group members of YIP had decisive majority in the Panchayats, the tendencies of simply ratifying the resolution prepared by Sarpanch continued. Third, the influence of vested interests continued in the Panchayats, and the union members are not able to counter such influences. Fourth, the decisions on funds allocation did not correspond to the promises made by the YIP union members before the elections, and also to the needs and aspirations of the people. Fifth, not all the members (especially women) attended the meetings. But, YIP union members have not initiated any measures to arrest such phenomena. Sixth, in some of the Panchayats, the records were not handed over to the newly elected Panchayats by the former President. But, the YIP union members neither took up this issue nor pressed for passing the resolution seeking the same. Seventh, although the bureaucracy of Gram Panchayats are encroaching into the space of members (and even Sarpanch), no attempts were made against such unhealthy practices. Eighth, some of the Gram Panchayat members (especially women) belonging to YIP functioned as name-sake members to their male relatives. A graphic description of a meeting of a Gram Panchayat (for which the author also attended) provides many pointers about the limitations of reservation policy in empowering women. The Sarpanch to this Gram Panchayat is a woman belonging to the YIP union, who sat in a corner and remained passive throughout the meeting. A few of the decisions relating to the Panchayat were taken not in the meeting but outside by a small group of influential members. The members belonging to YIP unions, instead of opposing the outside meeting, were party to such decisions! Suvarchala's paper provides many pointers about the degree of empowerment that political reservation can confer, the extent of participation of newly elected members and the limitations that the NGOs may confront in the process.

The NGOs wanting to facilitate linkages between their target group and the PRIs need to address these issues very urgently. Effective linkages with PRIs become difficult for those NGOs which adopt service delivery approach to development, which adopt antagonistic attitude towards the state, and which do not work towards lobbying and advocacy through networks. Webster suggests a dual track approach to NGOs, "providing qualitative development inputs to the people, and influencing the government policies through networks". Bhat argues that unless the NGOs are self-reliant, it is difficult for them to have critical collaboration with the government. This raises a larger issue relating to dependence on foreign funding and the implications that it has on democratisation and legitimacy of NGOs. This also raises issues relating to sustainability and self-reliance of NGOs. This volume does not go into the details of these issues as they are beyond its immediate scope.

NOTES

1. Some of the notable programmes implemented in the past were Community Development Programme (CDP), Land Reforms Programme, National Rural Employment Programme (NREP), etc. Some of the current programmes of national importance are Integrated Rural Development Programme (IRDP), Jawahar Rozgar Yojana (JRY), Minimum Needs Programme (MNP), Development of Women and Children in Rural Areas (DWCRA), etc. For a critical review of these programmes, see Rajsekhar and Namerta (1994).
2. Consists of Commercial Banks, Regional Rural Banks and Cooperatives.
3. The contributing factors to this are as follows:
   * Public institutions which are established with a clear objective of giving support to the poor households are not reaching them because of lack of congruence between the recipient system and delivery system.
   * The failure to mobilise the poor to demand services and to obtain help from the government is resulting in very little interaction with the beneficiaries, and failure of delivery systems. In the absence of effective organisations, the poor could not obtain their due share from these programmes.
   * The poor are handicapped in responding to these signals in the absence of capabilities and pressure groups of their own.
   * The flow of full benefits to the poor is being undermined with the involvement of contractors, middlemen or intermediary agencies. This is happening in spite of guidelines formulated to involve agencies capable of ensuring people's participation such as Gram Panchayats, village institutions, NGOs or concerned departments themselves, in implementing the community works/programmes.
   * Problems of corruption, diversion and execution.
4. For more details, see Rajasekhar (1998d).

5. A study of ideological pre-dispositions of about 100 members in seven Gram Panchayats concludes that although discursive ground is shifting, the rich peasants do not tolerate a democratic and enlightened departure (Lieten 1996).
6. For more details, see, Webster (1992a and 1992b).
7. For an analysis of Karnataka experiment, see, Aziz (1993). Also, see, Bhargava and Sivanna (1990), Bhargava and Vidya (1992), Chandrasekhar and Inbanathan (1991), Government of Karnataka (1989), Ray (1987), and Ray and Jayalakshmi (1987).
8. The term 'Target group' is not liked by some of the NGO activists. By target group we mean, women, Details and Adivasis. Within this category, the emphasis would be more on the landless, small and marginal farmers.
9. The grassroots NGOs could be either local based, working in a single and small project location, or be working in multiple project areas in different districts, states and regions covering a larger population.
10. For an elaborate discussion on how this change occurred in the specific context of NGOs in Kerala and Andhra Pradesh, see, Rajasekhar (1998b).
11. It is to be, however, noted that these are only comparative advantages. Often, the strengths of NGOs are discussed in comparison with the government and political parties. Another point is that these are potential advantages and that not all the NGOs are successful in achieving them.
12. Most often, NGOs take up a situational analysis and need assessment before initiating any development activity though the rigour with which such exercises are carried out may vary across the NGOs, But, a starting point in the case of most of the grassroots NGOs is the articulation of the problems of the community in their project location.
13. The geographical area of the NGOs tends to be small (Rajasekhar 1998a; Farrington *et al.*, 1993; Rajasekhar 1998b). Such a small geographical area enables the NGOs to be flexible. Methods and practices of formulation, implementation and monitoring of the programmes and style of working can easily be modified to suit the needs and aspirations of the community with which they are working, and changing rural conditions. Being small, NGOs rarely face the problems of hierarchy and bureaucracy that restrict the government departments. NGOs can respond swiftly and efficiently to local demands. Being locally based, they are aware of the local environment and are responsive to it.
14. The 'goal confusion' is one of the important contributing factors for the limited success of the government initiated programmes in India. On the other hand, the NGOs normally have one principal goal, which could be poverty alleviation, mobilisation of the marginalised section to access government programmes, etc. The NGOs adopt innovative and participatory methods and practices to achieve the goal.
15. The methods and practices adopted in formulation and implementation of NGO development programmes, selection of the target group, provision of services, etc., are relatively independent of the local power structures. This

contributes to the target group participation and success of the programmes. The evidence on the autonomy of NGO programmes is, however, mixed; studies noted that while NGO programmes enjoy relative independence as far as local power structures are concerned, they are influenced by donor and government policies (Rajasekhar 1998a).

16. The targeting is relatively good in NGO programmes. The studies reveal that 80 to 100 per cent of the target group in NGO project areas come from the poor categories as compared to only 60 to 70 per cent in government programmes (Murthy 1998). On the positive side, NGO 'development programmes have been most effective in the case of those poor with some initial endowment base. The NGOs are, however, not very successful in enabling the poorest among the poor, with very little endowment base to begin with, to expand the means to overcome poverty (Rajasekhar 1996; Rajasekhar 1998b; Murthy 1998).
17. See Rajasekhar (1998c), Kothai (1994) and Sangitha (1990).
18. It is difficult to estimate the exact number of NGOs engaged in development work today. One estimate is based on the registration with the Ministry of Home Affairs. For receiving any kind of assistance from international donors, NGOs should get themselves registered under the Foreign Contributions Regulation Act (FCRA), 1976, with the Ministry of Home Affairs. There are about 20,000 NGOs registered under FCRA. Even if one assumes that 50 per cent of them are active in rural and urban development, the number is large. There are also NGOs, without FCRA registration, which undertake developmental activities with assistance from the government and local contribution. If we include these organisations, the number would be much higher.
19. There is a debate on this. See, Webster (1995b: 407-8).
20. There is considerable disagreement as to where to draw the boundaries of civil society with respect both to the state and to the private domain of the individual. There is also considerable disagreement as to what civil society is composed of and as to what its political role can be.
21. See, Kothai 1994; Sangitha 1990.
22. The ability of NGO development programmes to reach the poorest was limited both because of structural and technical reasons (Rajasékhar 1996: 92-5). A review of the studies by Farrington *et al.* (1937) also suggests that this is a widespread problem.
23. The NGO proges tended to be palliative. Namerta's (1995) study on NGO sponsored income generation programmes reveals that most of the NGOs could only facilitate the undertaking of subsistence activities, and income from such activities was either equal to or less than the existing wage income. These activities made difference to the people in so far as they could be undertaken during the lean season and that the problem of seasonal unemployment could be, to some extent, solved. The income from the economic activities promoted by the NGOs formed only a small proportion

of the total income of the member families. Riddel and Robinson (1992) argue further that such an impact would be a barrier to the most fundamental structural changes in the ownership of principal productive assets which are essential if significant economic and political changes are to occur. As a result, the programmes may have succeeded in alleviating poverty, but, failed to address the more fundamental issues of vulnerability of the poor (Hulme and Mosley 1996).

REFERENCES

Aziz, Abdul (1993). *Decentralised Planning: The Karnataka Experiment*. Sage: New Delhi.

Bhargava, B. S. and N. Sivanna (1990). Emerging Pattern of Leadership in Panchayati Raj System: Case Study of a Zilla Parishad in Karnataka. *Indian Journal of Administrative Science*, 1 (2).

Bhargava, B.S and K.C. Vidya (1992). Position of Women in Political Institutions (with Special Reference to Panchayat Raj System in Karnataka). *Journal of Rural Development*, 11 (5).

Bhat, M.K. (1995). NGDOs, PRIs and People's Empowerment. In D. Rajasekhar *et al.* (eds.), *People Centred Rural Development: NGDOs and Decentralised Government*. Bangalore: ISEC, CDR, BCO and NOVIB.

Chandrasekhar, B.K. and Anand Inbanathan (1991). Profile and Participation of Women Zilla Parishad and Mandal Panchayat Members: The Case of Karnataka. *Journal Rural Development*, 10 (5).

Edwards, Michael and David Hulme. (1992). *Making a Difference: NGOs and Development in a Changing World*. London: Earthscan.

Edwards, Michael and David Hulme, (eds.) (1995), *Non-Governmental Organisations—Performance and Accountability: Beyond the Magic Bullet*. London: Earthscan.

Edwards, Michael and David Hulme (1996). Too Close for Comfort? The Impact of Official Aid on Non-Governmental Organisations. *World Development*, 24 (6).

Farrington, John *et al.* (eds.) (1993). *The Reluctant Partners? Non-Governmental Organisations, the State and Sustainable Agriculture*. London: Routledge.

Government of Karnataka (1989). *Report of the Zilla Panchayat and Mandal Panchayat Evaluation Committee*. (Chairman: K S Krishnaswamy). Bangalore : Department of Rural Development and Panchayati Raj.

Hulme, David and Paul Mosley (1996). *Finance Against Poverty*. London: Routledge.

Kothai, Krishna (1994). Economic Impact of Rural Development Projects on Small Farmers. *Journal of Rural Development*, 13 (2).

Lieten, G.K. (1996). Panchayats in Western Uttar Pradesh: Namesake Members. A Paper presented at the Conference on *Modern South Asian Studies*, Copenhagen.

Mathew, George (1994). *Panchayat Raj: From Legislation to Movement*. New Delhi: Concept.

Moore, M. (1993). Good Government? Introduction, *IDS Bulletin*, 24 (1).

Murthy, R.K. (1998). *Indian NGOs, Poverty Alleviation and their Capacity Enhancement in the 1990s: An Institutional and Social Relations Perspective*. New Delhi: FES. Forthcoming.

Namerta (1995). Income and Employment Generation Programmes of NGOs at India. A Paper presented at a Workshop on *From Chit-Funds to Community Banking*. Bangalore: NOVIB.

Pai, Sudha (1998). Pradhanis in the New Panchayats: Field Notes from Meerut District. *Economic and Political Weekly*. xxxiii (18).

Pal, Mahi (1998a). Women in Panchayat: Experiences of a Training Camp, *Economic and Political Weekly*, xxxiii (4).

Pal, Mahi (1998b). Panchayats in Election Manifestos: A Comparative Analysis. *Economic and Political Weekly*, xxxiii (12).

PRIA (1991). *Voluntary Development Organisations in India: A Study of History, Roles and Future Challenges*. New Delhi: PRIA.

Rajasekhar, D. (1995). NGDOs, People and Decentralised Government in Karnataka. In D. Rajasekhar *et al.* (eds.), *People-Centred Rural Development: NGDOs and Decentralised Government*. Bangalore: ISEC, CDR, BCO and NOVIB.

Rajasekhar, D. (1996). Problems and Prospects of Group Lending in NGO Credit Programmes in India. *Savings and Development*, 20 (1).

Rajasekhar, D. (1998a). Rural Development Strategies of NGOs. *Journal of Social and Economic Development*, 1 (2). Forthcoming.

Rajasekhar, D. (1998b). *Impact of Micro-Finance Programmes on Poverty and Gender Equality: Evidence from Indian NGOs*.

Rajasekhar, D. (1998c). *Non-Governmental Organisations (NGOs): Opportunities and Challenges*. Bangalore: SOSWA.

Rajasekhar, D. (1998d). *Professor G. Parthasarathy's Writings on Indian Rural Economy in Transition*. Jaipur: Printwell.

Rajasekhar and Lini Nair (1995). Networks among NGDOs in Karnataka. In D. Rajasekhar. *et al.* (eds.), *People Centred Rural Development: NGDOs and Decentralised Government*. Bangalore: ISEC, CDR, BCO and NOVIB.

Rajasekhar, D. and Namerta (1994). Wage Labour in the Agricultural Sector. in Sarath Davala (ed.), *Unprotected Labour in India: Issues and Concerns*. New Delhi: FES.

Ray, Amal (1987). New Panchayat System in Karnataka — Elections and After. *Economic and Political Weekly*. xxii (7).

Ray, Amal and K. Jayalakshmi (1987). Zilla Parishad Presidents in Karnataka: Their Social Background and Implications for Development. *Economic and Political Weekly*, xxii (42 & 43).

Riddel, R. and Mark Robinson (1992). The Impact of NGO Poverty Alleviation Projects: Results of the Case Study Evaluations. *Working Paper No. 68*. London: Overseas Development Institute.

Robinson, M. (1993). Governance, Democracy and Conditionality: NGOs and the New Policy Agenda. In A. Clayton (ed.), *Governance, Democracy and Conditionality: What Role for NGOs?* Oxford: INTRAC.

Sangitha, S.N. (1990). Self-Employment Programme for Rural Youth: The Role of Non-Governmental Organisations (NGOs). *iimb Management Review*, 5 (2).

Stephen, F. (1990). *NGOs: Hope of the Last Decade of this Century*. Bangalore: SEARCH.

Webster, Neil (1992a). *Panchayat Raj and the Decentralisation of Development Planning in West Bengal*. calcutta : K.P. Bagchi.

Webster, Neil (1992b). Panchayat Raj in West Bengal: Participation for the People or the Party. *Development and Change*, 23 (4).

Webster, Neil, (1995a). A Conceptual Approach to NGDOs and Panchayat Raj in Rural Development. In D Rajasekhar *et al.* (eds.), *People Centred Rural Development: NGDOs and Decentralised Government*. Bangalore: ISEC, CDR, BCO and NOVIB.

Webster, Neil, (1995b). The Role of NGDOs in Indian Rural Development: Some Lessons from West Bengal and Karnataka. *The European Journal of Development Research*, 7 (2).

Westergaard, Kirsten (1995). NGDOs and Local Self-Government in Bangladesh. In D Rajasekhar *et al.* (eds.), *People centred Rural Development: NGDOs and Decentralised Government*. Bangalore: ISEC, CDR, BCO and NOVIB.

2

NGOs AND LOCAL GOVERNMENT: THE DEMOCRATISATION OF LOCAL DEVELOPMENT

NEIL WEBSTER

INTRODUCTION

In an earlier paper (Webster 1995b), originally prepared for a workshop held at the Institute for Social and Economic Change, Bangalore, in 1995, on the theme of NGOs and Local Government, I developed a case which went along the following lines.

The Indian state has, to a large extent, failed to bring about a pro-poor development in the country on the basis of centralised planning and an import substitution strategy. I did not go into the factors behind this failure, but the reasons must be seen to lie in the balance of economic and political forces within the country and not merely in external factors beyond India's control—terms of trade, etc. While this failure might not be comparable to that of some African or Latin American countries, the fact that some 350 million or more Indians continue to live in poverty fifty years after Independence in itself demands change.

The pressure for change has come from many directions, not least from the poor themselves, not necessarily in mass movements, but in electoral voting behaviour, protests, sporadic violence, and much more. It has also come from organisations representing the poor, not least NGOs (i.e., local NGOs who concentrate upon development), who pursue political mobilisation as a part of their development approach. Both their emergence and their activities bear witness to the change under way over the past 10 years or so in local development in India.

Pressure has also come from outside, from the World Bank, from other multilateral and bilateral donors, and co-financing agencies or northern NGOs. Furthermore, it has come not only from organisations whose focus is on economic development, but also from those concerned with the environment, human rights including those of women and minorities, democracy and good governance. One can also mention the pressure from the international world of private business and finance as India emerges as an important arena for direct foreign investment and a market for a growing number of consumer and capital products. This external pressure has actively pressed for and supported the reform process towards economic liberalisation and subsequently, political liberalisation.

The priority now is to bring about economic growth through infrastructural investment and sectoral reforms to remove the bottlenecks that hinder the functioning of markets. At the same time, it is argued that social sectors should be provided with support to develop the necessary human capital for such growth as well as to provide a safety net for those who cannot secure their livelihoods in the market in the short term due to their social and economic conditions.

The process of political liberalisation is aimed at supplementing and supporting the process initiated in the economic sphere. Decentralisation, reforms directed at introducing greater accountability and transparency into governance, the development of a more effective civil society in which non-state organisations and associations can bring the interests of the marginalised sections of the population into the policy arena and the decision-making process, are all held to be central to this process.

If one is to focus upon the institutional actors involved alone for a moment, then from the global down to the local it can be said that there are many agendas being pursued in the pressure for change. What is quite striking is that, despite the differences in perspectives and approaches, at the policy level, there has emerged a degree of apparent consensus as to the type of change required at the local level. This is reflected in what I would call a common 'discourse on the local'. It is a discourse where terms such as empowerment, rights, participation, decentralisation, local planning abound. It is a discourse where the issues of democracy, good governance and human rights are closely interwoven into the discussion of local development. It is in many ways a counter discourse in that it seeks to challenge the dominant economic and political nexus that has controlled the economy and the politics of India for most of the post-Independence period. The fact that it is a discourse constituted by actors with quite different perspectives, with differing aims and objectives, has tended to be neglected as the drive to bring about the inclusion of the local in the broader processes of development is pursued.

In my previous paper (Webster 1995b), I argued that NGOs had some difficulty in finding themselves in this shifting terrain or field of development. Issues that had previously been marginalised and for which they had campaigned, were now being taken up as priorities in donor strategy papers; funds were increasingly being made available not only from co-financing agencies, but from multilateral, bilateral and the Indian government itself. Donor-funded projects with government institutions as partners, were increasingly asking for NGO involvement. One consequence has been that the role of NGOs has been increasingly defined by other institutional actors for whom the NGOs' local status is but one of several factors shaping the design of policy manifesting itself in the form of country strategy papers, sector programmes and individual project interventions.

A consequence for NGOs, given their already diverse natures and agendas, is that they now risk being even further fragmented by the 'green pastures' they find opening up before them, as funds become increasingly available and their activities increasingly promoted.

I continued to argue that NGOs needed to take several steps back from the immediacy of the development situation that they found themselves in, with its pressure of finding funds and of 'doing' local development, and I suggested that they should re-examine their role and, in particular, their relationship to the state in both theoretical and practical terms. In other words, they needed to (re)locate themselves within this new development terrain.

Such an exercise requires a better understanding not only of the range of institutional actors operating within the arena of Indian development at different levels, but the relationships between them. These can be seen as essentially relations of power, the political and economic power that is wielded and expressed in terms of the conceptualisation, design and practice of development in India. The exercise also requires that NGOs critically examine their own natures: their organisational and management structures; their relationship to the poor and the organisations of the poor that they seek to facilitate; their role as an intermediary between the poor and the state institutions (elected and administrative); the consequences of their work for the poor not covered by their interventions; and their relationship to other NGOs and other local institutions.

My conclusion in my previous paper was to state that if NGOs could understand their limitations and better define their relationship to the poor, on the one hand, and to the state, on the other, then they should work at the local level to generate sustainable grassroots organisations while becoming through networking, corporate actors representing the interests of the poor and marginalised groups at the higher levels of state and policy making. In this way they could make the state a better developer through decentralisation that involves shifting development down to the local, but one that links the local into the state.

What I want to discuss in the rest of the paper are three dimensions of this work which I feel need to be taken further. The first concerns the politics of (re)connecting the local with the state, the second, with the question of identifying the poor, i.e., those towards whom NGOs should be directing their work, and the third is the question as to who is constituting the local in the name of the poor?

RECONNECTING THE LOCAL TO THE ARENA OF HIGH POLITICS

Reaching the local has become an important issue in the work of donors and governments today with the focus falling upon two forms of institutional development, in particular, the decentralisation of government and the expansion of local NGOs in development activities.

The former is more often than not advocated on the basis of bringing greater democracy in the forms of accountability and participation at the local levels which, if linked to a devolution of responsibilities for development planning and administration and provided with adequate financial resources, can bring about both more effective and potentially more equitable local development.

Panchayat Raj has become the focal point for decentralisation policy in India with the 73rd and 74th Amendments to the Constitution requiring that not only do the state governments bring in legislation to generate local government institutions in both rural and urban areas, but that they also establish State Finance Commissions with the purpose of developing the mechanisms by which the financial resources necessary for successful devolution of government can be secured. The importance of decentralisation to the current orthodoxy on development is clear from the importance attached to decentralisation by the multilateral and bilateral donors. The presence of the institutional means to reach the poor at the local level is one of the important factors for many of the donors when making their selection of which Indian states to focus upon, and decentralisation is frequently linked to good governance and other issues such as human rights at the macro-policy level.

In the case of the latter, local NGOs[1] have increasingly come to figure in what Robinson (1993) has described as the 'New Policy Agenda' as donor agencies, northern NGOs, and increasingly southern states seek to support the process of political liberalisation that is currently accompanying the economic liberalisation policies introduced over the past ten years or so[2].

There are many reasons as to why NGOs have become so popular. Not least, markets and private initiatives are seen as the most efficient mechanisms for achieving economic growth and for providing services to most people. Governments should, therefore, facilitate the market because of its cost effectiveness in reaching the poor and NGOs should be brought in to reach those not reached by the markets. Here, we see how aid supported liberalisation goes hand in hand with increased aid to NGOs by donors.

With respect to policies on decentralisation and on NGOs there has been an increased tendency to link democracy with development. What I would call the fetishism of democracy in that democracy is seen to bring development with it. Whereas twenty or thirty years ago it was argued first development then democracy, today, the order and the causality imputed has been reversed; first, democracy to bring better development[3]. Today, we, therefore, talk of empowerment, of participation, of building up a thriving civil society and similar needs from development interventions.

NGOs are central actors at the local level within this thinking. They can provide a counter-balance to the state and become important actors in the planning and carrying through of development whether that be through development programmes or the securing or defence of rights—human, minority, land, etc.

If liberalisation is the economic side of the New Policy Agenda, the decentralisation of government and the strengthening of civil society are the political sides of the agenda. As Edwards and Hulme (1995) write, the tendency is to see NGOs as the 'favoured child' of official agencies and something of a panacea for the problems of development—the 'magic bullet' that can be fired off in any direction, but will in some way find its target. However, the danger is that by being elevated to such a central role in the process of political liberalisation, NGOs risk being encouraged to assume roles for which they are poorly equipped at the expense of those comparative advantages they do possess in local rural development.

The first point that I wish to argue once again is that NGOs must resist the tendency to have their role determined for them in this way. That there is a need for NGOs, donors, advocates and activists to take an analytical step backwards and to begin with the premise that it is neither realistic nor desirable for NGOs to seek to provide an adequate alternative to the state or to constitute part of an ideological project challenging the state. Instead, they should approach NGO-state relations in terms of a collaborative rather than a competitive relationship.

If one steps back from seeing NGOs as part of the project of rolling back the state, the discussion then changes to one of how to make the state a better developer through the intervention and involvement of other actors, in this case, NGOs. The next step is then for NGOs to reconsider their development role and political strategy and to establish how best to intervene at strategic institutional points in the political system in order to adjust policy and shift priorities in the development practice of the state.

As I have argued previously (Webster 1995a), NGOs should pursue a twin track approach of, on the one hand, building an effective base for influencing government through advocacy, while, on the other hand, building sustainable organisations of people located around their particular socio-economic needs, but with the political ability to begin to effect the process of government and thereby development, from below. Such a strategy requires that NGOs should seek to locate themselves within the broader institutional field of development and to analyse their relationship to the different institutional actors involved.

Who are the institutional actors involved in rural development? Who has the ability to organise, to act or to influence development at the local level? With the stress on pro-poor development interventions, I would argue that different institutions possess different capabilities according to the level and the political basis of their engagement. The focus here is upon those institutions that possess agency in the field of poverty alleviation on the basis of their organisational or institutional nature. At the local level are the administrative and elected institutions of local government, i.e., the local state, and then a range of local non-state organisations—local NGOs, community organisations, and people's organisations. While the former are formally constituted by the state through legislation and state practice, the relationship of the latter group to the state varies considerably.

The local we can characterise as the spatial location of low (everyday life) politics in contrast to the macro-level of high (state) politics. In studying the relationship between high and low politics, we can quickly recognise that it is not merely a relationship between the local and the macro in terms of scale and level, many institutions at the local level are in fact constituted at the macro, local state institutions, for example. Therefore, we must examine the linkages in terms of not only vertical linkages but lateral linkages as well. Furthermore, a local institution originally constituted on the basis of one set of relationships with the local and macro-institutions, might well change over time to another as policies change and new development practices emerge. Local NGOs have been particularly prone to this shifting of roles in India.

As discussed above, the development practice of the Indian state and of external donors is increasingly involving local NGOs. Their incorporation into development planning and practice, their registration for the receipt of government and foreign funds, and similar developments have in many ways led to a formalisation of their relationship to the state and thereby their role in development. One consequence of this has been that NGOs are increasingly being constituted from above rather than from below. This is most clearly witnessed by the growth in the number of NGOs. The availability of donor and government funds for NGOs must be seen as a principal factor in this growth. Most of these 'new' NGOs are organisations that have little to do with grassroots or community-based organisations. To the contrary, the 'rooting' of the NGO to a particular group of 'beneficiaries' more often than not occurs after the NGO has been established, its conceptual approach towards development defined, and its core members appointed. This reflects the earlier statement that NGOs should be seen as private organisations with clients and as distinct from grassroots organisations. NGOs are also registered organisations with respect to their legal and funding status.

The linking of local NGOs to the state and donors has been particularly important in shaping the degree and type of agency possessed by the NGOs. On the one hand, it can be argued that there is a greater political space for NGOs because of the legitimation afforded to them through changes in state policies and the provision of resources. On the other hand, the political nature of their role, i.e., the type of agency, has been increasingly constrained by the very process of becoming actors within the development practice of the state and donors.

The current development status of local NGOs can be contrasted with that of local grassroots organisations, sometimes referred to as people's organisations. Caste-based associations of agricultural labourers, local irrigation user groups, or environmental and farmers' social movements exist in a grey zone between acceptance by external agencies in that they are seen to be reflecting popular interest and as potential instruments in bringing about a more sustainable development, and rejection on the basis of the challenges to authority and to the wider development interests of the state and the national economy that they often express and espouse.

In an ideal situation, the potential roles of the state and of local organisations in bringing about a pro-poor orientation in development can be presented in thc following way (Chart 2.1)

The argument presented in Chart 2.1 is that there is a potential complementarity of roles existing between the state, local state institutions and non-state organisations in the field of poverty alleviation and the mobilisation of the poor. It makes the critical separation between the local or micro-level and the macro-level, between what we might call the arena of centrally organised country-wide poverty reduction programmes and interventions that focus more upon local groups and individuals who are poor.

While local institutions can be agents for centrally launched anti-poverty programmes directed at the large groups of the poor—women, share-croppers, agricultural labourers, landless, the illiterate, the under-nourished, etc.—they can also be agents for

CHART 2.1 : POTENTIAL ROLES OF THE STATE AND LOCAL ORGANISATIONS IN BRINGING ABOUT PRO-POOR ORIENTATION IN DEVELOPMENT

Level of intervention/ engagement	*Type and Level of Institution*		
	State	*Local State (Administrative and Elective)*	*NGO*
Macro	Infrastructure investment, human capital investment (health, education, etc.), credit programmes and so on. Policies directed at the redistribution of the benefits of economic growth. Policies directed at generating more participatory local politics.	Local implementation of macro-programmes Local participation in planning to provide greater input from the local levels into future policy and planning. Local lobbying of needs from existing macro-programmes.	Local implementation of macro-programmes. Local interpretations or variations in macro-programmes. Local implementation of international donors' aid programmes.
Micro	Primarily in changing individuals' and local groups' abilities to negotiate in key markets and to secure their entitlements.	Local input into planning formulation and implementation including the local distribution of benefits.	Projects designed to meet local problems identified through P.R.A., etc.
	In particular, legislation concerning rights with respect to land, tenancy, minimum wages, and in areas of minority rights, women's rights and so on.	Local problems resolved with the tools provided from macro interventions.	Projects for the local marginalised and underprivileged i.e., those without a political or developmental patron as they are seen to offer no reciprocal gift such as important electoral votes.

local groups of the poor who not only constitute part of these large groupings, but also face specific localised forms of poverty, for example, landless tribal women. In this example, different forms of economic, religious and gender disadvantage overlay one another to generate a local matrix of vulnerabilities, each of which can be a cause for poverty. Collectively, they present a social group of the poor that macro-level interventions cannot handle, and many institutions have great difficulty with.

It is not merely a problem at the level of policy, but more significantly it is a political problem in that the very economic and social relations that generate such a social constellation of poor often render its members as political liabilities or at least without political patrons. In the case of a democratic government that is dependent upon electoral support, should the ruling party seek to intervene through local government institutions, it can risk alienating a coalition of local interests that will threaten its local democratic survival. Ironically, therefore, democracy, and decentralised democracy, in particular, can fundamentally undermine the ability of the state to reach such local groupings of the poor. It is in this particular context, very much the Indian context, that it is suggested that the NGOs possess a greater potential to be poverty-oriented at the local level due to their political nature.

As stated, the situation presented in Chart 2.1 is an ideal one and it assumes that all the actors could be in agreement as to what constitutes desirable development and that they are willing to work towards shared objectives to achieve that development. Let us say that an acceptable long term development objective is economic growth with a strong pro-poor orientation to be secured through the good governance based upon effective, transparent and accountable administration and with political representation secured for all sections of the population. The above model would require that such an objective be accepted by all of the actors. In reality, such a situation is unlikely. Too many other factors influence the actors' agendas: bureaucratic traditions and practices, political interests, competing economic interests including budget allocations, and many more. Nevertheless, the potential for greater coordination around a pro-poor economic development can be located by such a model and NGOs can thereby not only locate their own specific roles, but also seek to bring other institutional actors to take up their respective roles.

There is a fundamental underlying premise in the above, namely, that the role of local NGOs is not merely to carry out local development projects whether it is on their own premises or on behalf of the state or a donor. The more important role for the local NGOs is to take up the task of bringing the local into the macro arena, into the arena of high politics where decisions are made, policies selected, and programmes designed. Where political parties fail in this, as is the case for most of India, then it must be the task of other actors to represent the local, to bring its interests and needs into policy and decision-making arenas at higher levels. NGOs can and should take this task seriously on behalf of the poor and marginalised whom they claim to work for at the local level. Such a premise is to take the argument concerning NGOs' comparative advantage beyond the now standard discussions of those inherent in their organisation and management structures, towards an argument concerning the broader need for an active civil society in a developing country. In other words, a shift from an institutional focus to a systems focus. However, for NGOs to develop a better understanding as to what their role should be within a broader developmental context, not least its political relationship to the state and other actors at different levels, it needs to have a clearer understanding of the purpose for which it is working.

POVERTY AND THE POOR

The abstract presentation of different roles above and the argument that local NGOs have a role in reconnecting the local with the macro processes of governance are based upon the premise that there can be a degree of agreement as to the long term overarching priorities of development.

In a country such as India, where poverty remains so pervasive and persistent a phenomenon, then poverty reduction must be such a priority objective and, therefore, central to NGOs' thinking and practice. In the case of poverty reduction, it is currently the case that disagreement is not with the aim, but with the means by which it can be achieved. With respect to the latter, it is also to be recognised that there is a growing awareness that both economic growth and redistribution have to be present in the policies pursued. Because of the status of poverty in current development thinking and the fact that the debate is more open, less ideological, than perhaps it has ever been before, it has created a political space in development practice and policy formulation that NGOs are in a position to utilise. It requires, however, that they maintain a clear sight of the poverty reduction goal at a general level and use this as a basis for locating themselves with respect to, and working with, other actors at both local and higher levels. It does require that NGOs also maintain a clear understanding of what they actually are—private organisations with clients designed to achieve a specific set of goals. The clients should be the poor, but who are the poor and how can NGOs be better at identifying the poor to target their activities towards?

There are presently two main approaches to the identification of poverty and thereby, the poor: the objective assessment approach and the people's perception of poverty each with their particular methodologies (Baulch 1996). These must be understood to be very much context specific both as to the particular forms that poverty takes and as to the cultural understanding as to what constitutes poverty in a given society. This leads on to the distinction between absolute poverty and relative poverty. Poverty is absolute when physical survival is at risk. Relative poverty is the failure to meet the living conditions held to be minimal or normal within a given culture or locality.

The continuous debates and discussions concerning the constitution of poverty, not least on the measurement of poverty and the location of a poverty line, have influenced a growing number to argue that poverty in itself is an inadequate concept. Not least, it often leads to a too simplistic approach to the analysis of poverty and to the design of poverty reduction programmes. Today, we speak of vulnerability, dependence, powerlessness, isolation, alienation, insecurity, the vocabulary is being extended all the time. But what these terms do carry in their meaning is the sense that poverty is more than a lack of assets or income, that structures are involved and that factors such as rules, norms, land relations, gender relations, etc., place and reproduce people in a disadvantaged position i.e., structural poverty.

Such terms can help in leading one to explore the factors that give rise to 'local social constellations of the poor' and in providing insights as to how the poor can be active in contesting and affecting the processes that give rise to their condition. By adopting a relational approach, one counterposes poverty to wealth, the poor to the non-poor. One recognises that the poor are actors who are not only having coping practices, but are also constantly seeking to change their condition through strategies designed to weaken their vulnerability, to provide greater security. These can range from individual strategies of migration through to forms of collective mobilisation (cooperatives, social movements, etc.). Recognition of the poor's own practices in the face of poverty mirrors the shift in thinking away from interventions that seek to drag the poor into an on-going process of economic growth whether through trickle down or some other externally initiated process.

It is not possible here to provide any easy answers as to how to identify the poor. It remains an area of considerable disagreement between researchers. Shifts towards a greater focus upon the identification of the poor and the issue of targeting in development projects have been greatly aided by the fact that some forms of poverty and resistance to the causes of poverty have been very visible, but the danger here is of working only with the visible poor. One major problem with this is that it ignores the time dimension and, for example, excludes those who are not amongst the poorest of the poor today, but may well be tomorrow.

Nevertheless, if one is to try to establish a working definition as to who the poor are, then the following might be a valid starting point: the poor are those who lack the physical assets and means that would provide a better economic and social condition—land, employment, food, income, capital, education, housing, clean drinking water, good health, literacy, low infant mortality, longevity of life, etc. Secondly, the poor are those who are vulnerable due to their identity (ethnicity, gender, religion, caste, age), due to their relationship to the key means for reproducing their lives (land, work, education, political services, development programmes, etc), due to their 'natural situation' (geographical, environmental). Finally, the poor are those who currently lack the means not to be poor and the power to change that situation.

If one then seeks to combine the objective and perceptive approaches towards locating poverty then it might be along the following lines: female headed rural households (due to male out migration) are identified as having a higher than average incidence of low assets, low consumption, low school attendance of children. Regionally, the data shows this to be a greater problem in forest regions where the majority of the population are classified as 'tribals' or indigenous ethnic groups. When meetings are held in these localities, women in the group meetings speak of sexual harassment, inability to obtain formal credit, lower agricultural wages than male workers, less opportunity for work and the negative or discriminatory attitudes and practices of officials and traders towards them in their interactions. They list the problems of poor drinking water, lack of schools and teachers for their children, lack of bus transport in their localities. At the same time they speak of labour sharing practices in their cultivation, of their knowledge and traditional engagement in minor forest products, of the traditions of younger women working in labour gangs for harvesting and transplanting rice in neighbouring districts. A profile thereby begins to emerge of not only the problems (i.e., their condition) but of some of the relations that make them so vulnerable (gender, land, labour, ethnicity, their peripheral location in political and developmental terms, and so on).

At the same time, the profile includes examples of organising practices at the household level, on the basis of gender, locality, work or knowledge, which might provide a basis for intervention, e.g., securing improved access to forests and facilitating their engagement in non-timber forest production and trade. More indirect aid in the form of drinking water, creches with food and medical support for young children, improved roads, etc., can also help facilitate the women engage in other practices that reduce their vulnerability. Finally, a credit and savings scheme can build upon the existing cooperation amongst women and link into support for their other activities.

It is not that the 'tribal' women have been simply categorised as poor and, therefore, targeted with aid. What the above example attempts to show is the need for a multi-dimensional concept of poverty when thinking about poverty and for the utilisation of both quantitative and qualitative methodologies when seeking to explore poverty.

For NGOs, the growing tendency is to become service providers on behalf of the state or donor agencies. In so doing, they become implementors of programmes or projects in which the design and identification phases have been established prior to the NGO involvement and there remains only a limited room for manoeuvre in the actual implementation of the project or programme by the NGO. The inadequacy of the conceptualisation of poverty in many of these programmes is surprising. Recent research suggests that despite the growing stress placed upon poverty reduction in bilateral and multi-lateral donors aid portfolios, little by way of conceptual thinking concerning poverty comes into the programmes and projects that they support[4]. Futhermore, much of the practice of aid intervention, not least the organisation and management of aid provision from project level up to country strategy level is non-conducive to the promotion of effective poverty reduction or, for that matter, the involvement of the poor in the identification, design, implementation, monitoring or assessment of aid projects. Ironically, much that the donors claim to be innovative and effective in their approach to poverty reduction is based upon a critique of developing states' own poverty reduction attempts. The present picture is, therefore, far from promising.

IN THE NAME OF THE POOR

This brings me to a final point I wish to take up here, namely, who is constituting the local? This might appear a somewhat abstract question, but the reality concerning the growing role of NGOs in development requires that we consider the possibility that the local in which so much aid is now being invested might well be more the product of the international development discourse and the development policies and funding that emanate from that discourse. It might well be that NGOs are becoming part of a broader project in which development policy and development theory come together and construct the very object that they take as their focus, that is the local. The local then becomes a creation of development academics, donor agencies, and consultants' images of the local. Researchers and NGO activists need to ask themselves whether this 'local' is something that can be accepted. For example, is it a local that reflects the structural relations of land, labour, gender, and caste that we know from decades of village studies in India? Is it the local that the villager, migrant labourer, or slum dweller would herself/himself describe and present if asked?

The local has been taken up in the name of the poor. For many, the local is the best point at which to start out on the process of helping the poor. Local institutions and organisations are currently part of the localisation of development. On the one hand, they are seen to represent the antithesis of the centralised state; it is the location of individuals that can and should take control of their lives without external agencies determining their development. On the other hand, appealing to a somewhat different set of political and philosophical beliefs, the local is where one finds collective forms of action: from social movements through to foot-dragging and non-compliance. Here, local organisations are the focus for a reemergence of interest in cooperatives, in sustainable, indigenous forms of resource management, it is at the local level one locates peasant resistance, where the subalterns' voices can be heard.

NGOs, in many ways, correctly, have been seen to be implicitly rooted in the local. They are often seen to speak the same language as the subalterns and therefore, to be able to speak on their behalf. Proximity to the poor, advocates of self-help by the poor, flexible and experimental in management and organisation practices, people-to-people organisations, even more cost effective, NGOs are seen to possess many fine characteristics.

With so much responsibility apparently placed upon NGOs, the task of retaining their pro-poor orientation in practice and not just in name is a difficult one. However, if (i) they critically examine their nature in terms of their relationship to other actors and in particular to the state; (ii) they retain a clear sight of what their fundamental objectives are *vis-a-vis* the poor and poverty reduction; and (iii) they remain aware of the fact that the local does not merely exist, but is constituted through the actions of many actors, and one of the roles of NGO is to ensure that the local as experienced by the poor is re-introduced into the politics of government; then NGOs can hope to continue to play an important role in poverty reduction.

NOTES

1. Here, we are using the term NGO to describe intermediary organisations engaged in funding or offering other forms of support to communities and other organisations and Grassroots Organisations (GROs) to describe membership organisations of various kinds. The most important distinction lies in their accountability structures. NGOs in the south are primarily accountable to their boards and to the funding agencies. The requirement to register with the state, often linked to the receipt of foreign and government funds, also carries a degree of accountability, but there is little accountability to the beneficiaries, i.e., NGO 'Clients'. GROs are primarily accountable to their members.
2. See Chapter 1, in Edwards and Hulme (1995).
3. For example, Huntington's (1968) argument that it was not so much the type of government, but the strength of government that is crucial as found in his classic work.
4. For example, see Cox, *et al.* (forthcoming).

REFERENCES

Baulch, B. (1996). The New Poverty Agenda: A Disputed Consensus. *IDS Bulletin*, 27(1).

Cox, A., S. Folke., L. Schulpen and N. Webster. *Do The Poor Matter? A Comparative Study of European Aid for Poverty Reduction in India*. London: ODI. Forthcoming.

Edwards, M. and D. Hulme (1995). *Non-Governmental Organisations: Performance and Accountability*. London: Earthscan.

Huntington, S. (1968). *Political Order in Changing Societies*. New Haven: Yale University Press.

Robinson, M. (1993). Governance, Democracy and Conditionality: NGOs and the New Policy Agenda. In A. Clayton (ed.), *Governance, Democracy and Conditionality: What Role for NGOs?* Oxford: INTRAC.

Webster, Neil. (1995a). The Role of NGDOs in Indian Rural Development: Some Lessons from West Bengal and Karnataka. *European Journal of Development Research,* 7(2).

Webster, Neil (1995b). A Conceptual Approach to NGDOs and Panchayat Raj in Rural Development. In D. Rajasekhar *et al.* (eds.), *People-centered Rural Development: NGDOs and Decentralised Government*. Bangalore: ISEC, CDR, BCO and NOVIB.

3

INTERFACE BETWEEN NGOs AND DECENTRALISED GOVERNMENT*

ABDUL AZIZ

The purpose of this paper is to present a few thoughts on the capacity building role that the NGOs can take upon themselves in the context of the need for strengthening the decentralised governments, especially the PRIs. Even though my training is in economics, over the past few years, I had the opportunity to familiarise myself with the basic issues involved in the Panchayat Raj system and learning from Panchayat members whom we are training in our Institute for the past two years. I have also learned somewhat about the problems of planning and implementation at the grassroots level through field visits in Karnataka.

The PRIs are today seen as third level governments, thanks to the 73rd Constitutional Amendment Act of 1992. We have today the Union government at the national level, the state governments at the state level and the Panchayats at the grassroots level. The latter have the basic responsibility of governing and planning at the local level. Local level governance and planning are thus the basic functions of the PRIs. If these are their basic functions, the question is, what activities operationally are they supposed to engage themselves in? To state, in brief, they are expected to identify the needs of the people and the local resources, match the needs of the people with the available resources, formulate projects to be implemented by the people's representatives in collaboration with the bureaucracy. In this paper,

* The Author is grateful to Dr. D. Rajasekhar for useful comments on the earlier version of this paper.

while elaborating upon the problem of planning and governance processes, the reference is to the lowest level of the PRI bodies, i.e., the Gram Panchayats.

Given this responsibility of governance and planning, what is the track record of Gram Panchayats in the southern states, particularly in Karnataka? Based on my experience as a member of the Karnataka State Finance Commission and as a faculty member organising and directing a training programme for the Panchayat members in Karnataka, two important deficiencies have come to my notice in respect of PRIs. One, the members of the Panchayats are not able to mobilise the required resources. They are not able to impose and collect taxes, raise sufficient amount of resources through any other means including voluntary contribution from the people which is one of the sources of income for the PRIs under the Karnataka Panchayat Act of 1993.

This point may be illustrated by presenting some statistical data. As state-wise data on the income structure of the grassroots Panchayats are difficult to come by, we have presented information about the average income pattern of selected Gram Panchayats in Karnataka (Table 3.1). From this table it is evident that the Gram Panchayats have been operating with low levels of funds. The average annual income available to the Panchayats is Rs. 1.84 lakhs and Rs 2.52 lakhs respectively in the years 1994-95 and 1995-96. By any standard, this amount is quite inadequate to carry out their responsibilities as local governments. Secondly, on an average, tax revenues of the selected Gram Panchayats are about 32 per cent in 1994-95 and 24 per cent in 1995-96 of the Panchayat income. Even if a liberal year figure is taken, it accounts for a third of the total income of the Gram Panchayats. The non-tax revenue is about 7 per cent of the income and an equal proportion of income comes from miscellaneous sources. This means that the Gram Panchayats by their own effort raise about 45 per cent of their resources and depend on government grant to a large extent—this dependence in some Panchayats going up to 80 per cent. The inability of the Gram Panchayat members to raise own resources is due to the fact that they are very close to people. Being very close to people, they cannot impose taxes

TABLE 3.1: INCOME PATTERN OF SELECTED GRAM PANCHAYATS IN KARNATAKA DURING 1994-95 AND 1995-96

(in Percentage)

Source of Income	Chikmagalur *District*						Hassan *District*				Bangalore *Rural Dist.*	Gulbarga *District*	Kolar *District*	*Average of the selected G Ps*	
	Jayapura		*Sollapura*		*Gudihalli*		*D Kallenahalli*		*Anemahal*		*C R Patna*	*T Sultanpur*	*Hulibele*		
	1994-95	*95-96*	*1994-95*	*1995-96*	*1994-95*	*1995-96*	*1994-95*	*1995-96*	*1994-95*	*1995-96*	*1994-95*	*1994-95*	*1994-95*	*1994-95*	*1995-96*
Tax Revenue	30.32	37.09	26.64	16.88	13.48	14.62	54.38	17.81	18.29	20.95	21.49	61.03	14.80	32.25	23.65
Non Tax Revenue	18.87	16.79	6.38	0.70	1.96	1.92	0.00	0.00	2.06	0.44	12.39	6.28	0.61	7.62	5.60
Miscell-aneous Income	23.43	0.60	0.00	27.42*	0.77	0.00	0.00	35.92*	23.65*	17.59*	2.72	0.00	14.21	3.34	15.82
Grants in-aid	27.39	45.42	66.99	55.00	83.80†	83.47	45.62	46.24	56.01	61.01	63.39	32.69	70.35	50.79	54.91
Total	100.00 (319)	100.00 (387)	100.00 (131)	100.00 (239)	100.00 (104)	100.00 (165)	100.00 (227)	100.00 (270)	100.00 (185)	100.00 (205)	100.00 (154)	100.00 (191)	100.00 (163)	100.00 (184)	100.00 (252)

NOTE:
+ – A large part of this is from entertainment tax.
† – Estimated figure
* Mainly opening balance and income from previous panchayats.
Figures in parentheses are in Rs. 1000.

and collect them with a rigorous drive. If they ever did so, there is a fear that they are not likely to be re-elected for the next term. Besides, under such circumstance, the Panchayat members will not be looked upon as the true representatives of the people who are expected to promote the interests and welfare of the community. This is the basic problem of grassroots level Panchayats.

The other deficiency is that the Panchayat members hardly participate effectively in planning and governance process. This is due to three reasons: one, as the funds available for planning are limited there is nothing much to plan with the limited funds. Under the circumstances, members lose interest in participating in the planning and governance process. Secondly, the Panchayat members lack skills required for planning and implementing the development programmes because they are not educated and not trained in the art of planning. Thirdly, most of them are illiterate, particularly those who come from weaker sections like SCs, STs, women etc. Since planning, implementation, monitoring, etc., are the frightening words as far as they are concerned such members tend to leave this job to the elite members. It is also possible that the latter discourage the illiterate and backward class members from fully participating in the process by their sheer dominance.

Given this situation, there is a great need for capacity building at the Panchayat level. Capacity building is being attempted by the government machinery by providing basic information, screening appropriate movies, organising speeches by dignitaries and training programmes. These attempts, however, have not fully helped the Panchayat members because these are 'hit and run' kind of attempts. Thus, the trainers may visit villages for a couple of days, talk to people, and then disappear. The result of which is that the clientele, namely, the Panchayat members, relapse back to their original position. Therefore, some kind of a sustained effort is needed for promoting not only skills of planning and implementation among the PRI members but also motivating them to give some special attention to resource mobilisation. It is in this context that we should see a definite role for the NGOs. NGOs are organisations of committed individuals and social workers who can go to, and live in the villages, if the situation so demands, and work with the people. These are the kind of people and institutions who can train the PRI members on a sustainable basis in the art of planning and implementing local level development projects. Therefore, it seems to me that the NGOs do have a very important role to play as far as capacity building of the PRI members is concerned.

Their role can be seen at three levels: one, they have to work with the people to promote latter's participation both in the development process and in the political process. In some states, such as in Tamil Nadu, people belonging to weaker sections are not motivated at all to contest for elections. In such cases, the NGOs are expected to take on the role of motivating weaker sections to contest for elections. This need arises because we have reservation for weaker sections of the population, who do not traditionally like to come out and work with members of other communities. So, the NGOs have to not only motivate such sections but also put courage into their minds to contest elections. They should also be educated to participate in the election process by exercising their franchise without fail.

Besides, the NGOs have to motivate people to participate in the planning and implementation processes by regularly attending Gram sabha meetings. Gram Sabha is an institutional structure that is available for the citizens to articulate their needs and aspirations. That is where they can say this is what we want and provide it. This is the forum where people are also expected to review the progress of the PRIs with regard to planning and implementation. In other words, in the Gram Sabha meetings people are not only expected to articulate their needs but also to critically review the work done by the PRIs. But experience has it that people's participation is very low in the Gram Sabha meetings. It is low in two senses: one, attendance is thin in the meetings because of lack of motivation among people. Also, people have a notion that only those who are interested in getting assistance under the various anti-poverty programmes should attend these meetings. They do not realise that they have greater responsibilities of participating in discussion about planning and reviewing the work of Panchayats. Secondly, not all of those present actively participate in discussion. It is not their presence as their participation in discussion that is important. Therefore, the NGOs have a special role in educating the citizens and in encouraging and equipping them with necessary skills of participation in Gram Sabha meetings.

NGOs should play a more constructive role in augmenting the Panchayat resources. They should urge and educate the Panchayat members to depend less on government grants by raising more of own resources by levying and collecting local taxes. Also, they should educate the Panchayat members on the various possible sources of raising non-tax revenues by building and developing income-yielding assets of the Panchayats. The good examples of Panchayats successfully doing so should be brought to their notice. Further, since there is always the possibility of citizens resisting imposition and collection of taxes, the NGOs are also expected to motivate people to contribute to Panchayat resources, by paying local taxes and user charges such as water rates, electricity charges,etc. And, people should be told that if resources are not available to the Panchayats, development process cannot be sustained and that they should pay for the benefits they get from the Panchayats. The NGOs can also motivate the people to make voluntary contributions in terms of labour and in other forms for supporting development programmes.

The second level where the NGOs have to contribute is at the Gram Panchayat level. The inputs to be provided to these bodies are information and initiating attitudinal changes among Panchayat members. Information has to be provided to the members on all aspects of Panchayat governance and planning because members are illiterate and have no exposure to law and other literatures. They should be told as to what exactly is their role in Gram Panchayats, how are they expected to participate in meetings and discussions, what are their rights, privileges and limitations. This is extremely necessary because they are expected to function more effectively as true representatives of the people. Secondly, attitudinal change has to be initiated regarding certain aspects of Panchayats. For example, we find that the male members are not very happy that the female members represented an interest along with them. The reservation of seats/executive positions to women of the order of 33 per cent in Karnataka has been resented on the ground that reservation at the Panchayat membership level is okay, but why at the executive level. Similarly, reservation to SC/ST members is also not welcomed by many because they feel that traditionally these groups are not entitled for administering the village affairs. In this context, there is a need to bring about attitudinal changes among members for their effective functioning in the Panchayats. They need to be told that in a democracy every section of the community should have access to decision-making process and that since the weaker sections are not in a position to come out on their own, there has to be a reservation policy to help them come out. This kind of attitudinal change can be imparted effectively to the people only by the NGOs since they have easier access to the people more than anybody else.

The third important input that needs to be given to the Panchayat members is skills of planning and implementation. When we say that the NGOs have to give planning skills to the Panchayat Raj members, we are not referring to the skills that are needed at the Planning Commission level which operates with technically sophisticated development models. Technical models are not required as a guide to promoting development in rural areas. All that needs to be given to them is firstly to make the members feel that as a representative of a particular village/ward he/she has to identify the needs of the area in terms of drinking water, school buildings, road connecting the village with the taluk, street lights, sanitation facilities, etc. Then help them to identify the resources that are available in the villages for being used to implement this particular project. List these needs and resources, present them before the Gram Panchayat to prioritise for actual implementation. Thus, the local level planning process is very simple consisting of the simple tasks of identifying the needs, identifying the resources, preparing a project, presenting it to the Panchayat emphasising the priorities for the area. Those projects which cannot be implemented due to lack of resources can be postponed for the subsequent year. This kind of development skills need to be imparted to the Panchayat members.

The NGOs have to build such capacities among the village bureaucracy too. The village bureaucrats are the ones who actually implement the programme which the Panchayat members would have formulated. Particularly, the Panchayat secretaries need to be told as to what they should do and how they should go about doing their jobs. They need some data, and they need information to understand what the village problems are. The NGOs can carry out a household survey regarding who exactly are the poor in the village and pass this information to the Panchayat bureaucracy. They can also prepare an inventory of amenities that are available in the villages, identify gaps and indicate how such gaps can be filled. This information will be extremely useful to the Panchayat members to work with. Also, the local developmental problems—problems relating to non-availability of rural infrastructure, skilled workers, capital, natural resource use and low productivities—should be identified and members briefed about. Imparting to members knowledge about how such problems should be tackled at the local level will be another useful activity of the NGOs.

Capacity building among Panchayat members, Panchayat bureaucrats and citizens will go a long way in promoting rural development. As we have stated above, the NGOs have to take upon themselves the role of building capacities among the various actors of rural development. However, there is a problem here. And that relates to the interaction between NGOs and Panchayats. It may be noted that at present there is absolutely no interaction between these two institutions. The reason is that the Panchayats view the NGOs with suspicion as competitors. The NGOs, on the other hand, being too much self-righteous, look upon Panchayats as institutions of vested interests and exploiters of the poor. With such a mind set it will be difficult to expect these institutions to work together as partners in rural development. Considering such a possibility it may be suggested that the NGOs and the Panchayats should meet more often and exchange views. Such meetings will go a long way in clarifying the positions taken by them and in resolving misunderstandings between them, if any.

4

SUSTAINABILITY AND LOCAL GOVERNANCE

M. K. Bhat

AN OVERVIEW OF NGOs IN INDIA

During the late 1960s and the early 1970s, a big section of the liberal and radical intelligentsia got attracted to the Marxist Frame of Analysis to understand the root causes of poverty and exploitation. One of the important causes of poverty was understood to be the class nature of society with the rich exploiting the poor. Those who had concern for the poor and exploited but anti-establishment in their attitude werc increasingly getting attracted to the class theory and class approach. The world was seen divided between two broad blocks, namely, socialist and capitalist, notwithstanding the conflicts and contradictions in each block. Most of all those who desired to work for the eradication of poverty and fight exploitation accepted Marxism as a guiding philosophy, and socialist model to seek solution to all the ills of the capitalist society.

In India, such a phenomenon saw a large number of radical youths and a section of intelligentsia following similar course during the late 1960s and the early 1970s. The issues such as gender, environment, human rights, sustainable development, etc., were not only not found in the political vocabulary but, on the other hand, were thought to be alien ideas imposed by the capitalist world.

The concept of development, confined essentially to the so called mainstream development, was more or less following western models under the guidance and control of the state in the name of democratic socialism but following state capitalism which exhibited anti-poor thrust from the start.

The pro-poor and pro-marginalised voluntary activities had charity and service motto essentially confining to education, health etc. Church, with resource support from the North and West, was on the lead in promoting such services with quality. Such processes contributed to communal harmony between the Christians and Hindus, notwithstanding the efforts of the Hindu communalists to divide them; this is in contrast with what has been happening between Hindus and Muslims.

By the mid 1970s, the impact of Marxism/Communism brought a split in the Church with the advent of liberation theology. Paulo Freire's (1972) *Pedagogy of the Oppressed* became the Bible for dissenters within the Church. Simultaneously, in India, the coming together of Lohiaites and Gandhians under Jayaprakash Narayan and launching of Total Revolution movement, the subsequent declaration of emergency rule, coming together of all from right to left—under the anti-emergency struggle, etc., brought in lot of permutations and combinations. Dissenters within the left, who started feeling the inadequacy of following only class approach combined with a desire to strengthen the grassroots level activity to improve the quality of life, started coming out of the Left movement to have more democratic and appropriate choices.

Thus, the late 1970s saw the convergence of the people coming out of the Church the convergence of the Left, the Gandhian and Lohiaites movements on the field of development at the grassroots with focus on awareness creation and conscientisation. With this, the late 1970s and the early 1980s saw a lot of youths with commitment to ideology following the course of social activism to influence the development process at the grassroots. While the traditional Left saw in such a development the hands of the Imperialism, the Church saw in it the danger of Communism. Such coming together was extensively facilitated with external donor support.

Pragmatism combined with the need to improve the life situation of the poor soon made people from all streams to talk of development by the mid 1980s. The fragmented, compartmentalised development work which still had charity and service orientation was soon replaced by the integrated development models by the late 1980s. The structural obstacles placed at each level of the activities and the need to influence the policies gave rise to the 'empowerment models' by the early 1990s. The gender justice, environmental concerns, human rights (more appropriately, in a country like India, the basic socio-economic-cultural rights), etc., were understood to be part and parcel of the structural aspects of the society which, apart from class, caste and ethnicity, also were responsible for the exploitation of the marginalised sections of the society. The external donors' pro-active role, the global events, etc., provided a macro-perspective to the grassroots work with the perspective of structural alleviation of poverty and exploitation through sustainable development processes by integrating gender, environment and human right concerns into the process. Together with this development, the NGOs developed the perspectives of the participatory processes (as against the top down and centralised approach of the political and governance system) and many started practising them at the grassroots to strengthen the self-management and grassroots democracy. Thus, from the charity-service and different ideologies of the early 1970s emerged the concept of sustainable development in the mid 1990s with quite a number of NGOs following this perspective. This, however, does not mean that all the NGOs in the country fall in the same category. Over the wide spectrum of NGOs in India one could find various types of NGOs explained above.

POSITION OF NGOs IN 1990s

Over the past one decade the number of NGOs in India have multiplied by manifold. It is estimated that over 15,000 NGOs, most of them with rural focus, are actively collaborating with external donors. From the position of untouchability (for the political parties) and suspicion, NGOs have now acquired legitimacy and credibility to a great extent[1] (notwithstanding the charges of corruption and lack of public accountability and transparency on some NGOs).

NGOs find a place in many government and semi-government policy and implementation bodies. With the failure of the state in reaching the poor and the marginalised[2] and with the lack of interest in the political parties in addressing the day-to-day life situation of the poor and marginalised, NGOs in India, like in many other southern countries, have come to play a very important role. As a part of civil society the NGO's role in micro-macro linkages and policy advocacy has become a dominant feature now.

To keep in line with the process of privatisation, the state has gradually been following the principle of social contracting with the NGOs in implementing its anti-poverty programmes (Robinson 1993), thus providing lot of space for the NGOs to collaborate with the governments in power. At the same time, the NGOs, together with the marginalised sections of the society, are actively involved in opposing the policies of the state and governments which are detrimental to the livelihood systems of the poor.

The structural adjustment, liberalisation and privatisation pursued under the New Economic Policy during the past half-a-decade have linked India to the process of globalisation. At the same time, market forces have destroyed the livelihood systems of the poor, as for example, in the case of the coastal belt[3].

While India's foreign exchange/balance of payment position seems to be much better, its poor and marginalised have been further marginalised, large scale displacement, feminisation of poverty (Deshpande and Deshpande 1992), increased rural-urban migration, widespread destruction of livelihood systems of the poor, etc., have increased with alarming speed. Recent National Sample Survey (NSS) data have indicated that the number of people living below the poverty line has increased in the post-reform period (Dev and Ranade 1997).

While there has been opposition from some corners of the political party spectrum, by and large, there is a consensus on the economic policies pursued. The difference is only on the speed and checks and balances! In such a situation, it is the NGOs, particularly those who are actively involved in micro-macro linkages and policy advocacy, who have stood by the people, and are now involved in opposing the wrong policies. Mass mobilisation, legal action and media campaign are now the recurring features of the day[4].

In such a situation, as explained above, making a distinction between development NGOs and Advocacy NGOs is a difficult proposition. All those NGOs who are genuinely involved in the process of strengthening the sustainable livelihood systems/ institutions of the people have to combine development work with sustainable models and policy advocacy[5].

In the initial stages, the NGOs thought that they could work with and/or influence political parties on people's needs and agenda. But their response was negative. They saw NGOs with suspicion. NGOs too contributed to develop antagonistic feeling by criticising the entire political party spectrum. Political parties, however, gradually added some of the agendas/issues because of the worry of losing their constituency, but not due to the genuine concern. Now, it is time for all the interested to join together on issues related to sustainability and livelihood, notwithstanding the differences and diversity. NGOs should initiate and give lead to strategic alliances in the interest of the poor and marginalised.

Thus, the position of the NGOs in the 1990s is very challenging. In the emerging scenario that would take the world to the New Millennia, the NGOs face the dual task of collaborating (critically) with the state and at the same time fighting its anti-people, anti-poor and anti-marginalised policies. Such a dual task cannot be discharged effectively unless the NGOs have autonomy based on the self reliance capabilities (Bhat 1995). NGO's sustained intervention will depend very much in future on their self-reliant capacity and local resource mobilisation.

SUSTAINABILITY AND GRASSROOTS MODELS

The paradigm of mainstream development indicates that this model is not sustainable in the ultimate analysis. Its anti-people, anti-women, anti-environment, anti-sustainable (etc.,) thrust have done irreversible damage and destruction. Yet, the process of globalisation is pursued with alarming speed notwithstanding the fact that those who opposed it are part of the governance of the country since 1996 Parliamentary Elections.

While opposing this destructive approach, one cannot wait (perhaps may not be possible in the foreseeable future) to see the reversal of this policy in the given global context. What is urgently needed is to develop and strengthen micro-level people-centered and self-managed models with potential for growth and whose sustainability will depend upon their ability to self-manage and to link to (and challenge if needed) the mainstream development processes from the position of strength. Grassroots level micro-banking systems[6], community resource management, collective and co-operative income generation activities, etc., are possible models. Local resource mobilisation, both human and material, micro-macro linkages and strategic alliances with interested actors and change agents in the civil society would provide sustainable strength against rapidly changing environment. Creating an enabling environment against rapidly changing socio-economic-political situation, and also against the destruction of livelihoods, is an urgent task since sustainability will depend upon social, political, financial, institutional and cultural factors.

FROM EMPOWERMENT TO POWER: GRASSROOTS DEMOCRACY AND PRIs

With the 73rd Constitutional Amendment making the PRIs to compulsorily function, new opportunities and challenges are opened up at the grassroots for the NGOs. Since the Gram Panchayat elections are supposed to be fought without any political party symbol (supposed to be a non-party event!), it provides a very good opportunity for the NGOs to educate and enable the poor to enter into the local level governance. The PRIs within the proximity of the people are within the reach of the people whereas higher level bodies are not as of now.

One-third reservation for women and one-third reservation for the socially oppressed and economically exploited Dalits make it possible to change the content of these local governance bodies. With proper education, training and strategies, it is possible for the enlightened and capable poor women and men to not only enter into these bodies democratically but also give new dynamism to the bottom-up development process. Further, this could make the PRIs pro-poor and pro-marginalised, thereby strengthening and activating the Gram Sabhas (village community). This could make the PRIs and elected members to discharge their responsibilities as people's representatives, enabling the poor to access local resources. Strengthening of these grassroots democratic bodies will have a cumulative effect on the body politics of the country!

While some NGOs have focused on this aspect of grassroots process, a large number have not realised the potential[7]. The NGOs, over the years, have promoted vast social infrastructure of the poor, the women, the Dalits, etc. Enabling them to influence the policies, enter into governance at least at the grassroots level and strengthening the local level democracy will go a long way to improve the life situation of the poor and empower them further. This will also go a long way in sustaining the initiative of the people for sustained growth and development. Thus, mere participation of women and the marginalised would not bring the desired changes (Box 4.1).

The sustainability of the grassroots level, people-centered, participatory and self-managed development processes will ultimately depend on the capability of the people in local resource mobilisation and influencing policy processes. Mere assertion of rights through social mobilisation and democratic pressure will not satisfy their basic and development needs. Entering the governance at the local level and bringing in a qualitative change in the local bodies in favour of the poor and marginalised could integrate equity principle and sustainability factor into micro-development processes. This, in turn, could strengthen the bottom-up development processes with its impact on the so-called mainstream development. The vast social infrastructure of the poor and marginalised, the women, the Dalits, the Adivasis, the agricultural labourers, etc., promoted by the NGOs all over the country exhibits such potential and possibilities explained above. However, transforming them into reality depends very much on the political initiative of the people which, in turn, depends on the perspectives with which NGOs organise them. The experiences of some of the NGOs in the states of Kerala, Karnataka, Andhra Pradesh and Tamil Nadu confirm such possibilities. Sharing of different perspectives and experiences will not only help to clarify many doubts but will also help to develop better strategies for the future.

BOX 4.1: WHO ARE EMPOWERED?

In one of the Panchayats in Anantapur District the Sarpanch seat was reserved for a SC woman. The union put up its candidate and the local political power centres selected the wife of one of the SC leaders as a rival candidate. Our (YIP) union was threatened and told that if the union candidate did not withdraw, on the day of the polling, union supporters would be prevented from voting. The union sought and got police protection.

The contest was very close and tense. The union candidate lost by 59 votes. That evening the husband of the winning candidate was garlanded and taken in a victory procession through the whole Panchayat. When the husband was asked where is the Sarpanch, he replied she is cooking at home.

The victory quite apparently was his not hers. This is an excellent example of how reservation is necessary but not sufficient to bring the oppressed to power.

If the women are not organised to fight for power with the support of their union they do not come to power but their husbands do. They are only there as puppets. What has changed? Nothing. This is not what YIP wants, YIP wants real social transformation.

Source: Bedi (1997: 207-8)

NOTES

1. This is evident from a large number of government programmes formulated to involve the NGOs. Reddy and Rajasekhar (1996), and Rajasekhar and

Reddy (1997) discuss the Central Government Programmes, and local development programmes, in detail.

2. For a detailed review of the development programmes, see, Rajasekhar and Namerta (1994).
3. For more details, see, Dharmaraj and Dharmaraj (1997).
4. Several interesting ways of advocating the cause of the poor are discussed in Joshi (1997).
5. For a discussion on the concept of advocacy, see, Joshi (1997).
6. Rajasekhar (1994 and 1997) discuss the problems and prospects in sustaining development work through micro-finance programmes.
7. A study of 16 NGOs in Karnataka shows that the NGOs chose to adopt four strategies with regard to interface with Gram Panchayats: (1) No engagement, i.e., a complete lack of interaction; (2) Limited engagement i.e., a non-political engagement, limited to cooperation in rural development programmes; (3) An indirect political engagement wherein the NGO facilitates the ability of the target group to self mobilise with respect of the PRIs; and (4) A direct political engagement in terms of actively seeking to have the target group members elected. A large number of the selected NGOs did not engage with PRIs or sought to adopt the strategy of limited engagement. Only two NGOs adopted the strategy of direct political engagement with PRIs. For details, see, Rajasekhar (1995).

REFERENCES

Bedi, Narinder (1997). PRIs and Social Transformation. In M.K. Bhat *et al.* (eds.), *Partners in Progress: Experiences of Voluntary Organisations in India*. Bangalore: DSI.

Bhat, M.K. (1995). NGDOs, PRIs and People's Empowerment. In D. Rajasekhar. *et al.* (eds.), *People Centred Rural Development: NGDOs and Decentralised Government*. Bangalore: ISEC, CDR, BCO and NOVIB.

Deshpande, Sudha and L.K. Deshpande (1992). New Economic Policy and Female Employment. *Economic and Political Weekly*. xxvii(4).

Dev, Mahendra S. and Ajit Ranade (1997). Poverty and Public Policy: A Mixed Record. In Kirit S. Parikh (ed.) *India Development Report*. New Delhi: OUP.

Dharmaraj, Jocob and Daisy Dharmaraj (1997). A Movement against Shrimp Industry. In M.K. Bhat *et al.* (ed.), *Partners in Progress: Experiences of Voluntary Organisations in India*. Bangalore: DSI.

Freire, Paul (1972). *Pedagogy of the Oppressed*. Harmondsworth, Middlesex, England: Penguin.

Joshi, S. (1997). What is Advocacy? An Overview. In S. Joshi *et al.* (eds.), *Experiences of Advocacy in Environment and Development*. Bangalore: DSI and NOVIB.

Rajasekhar, D. (1994). *Savings and Credit Systems of the Poor: Some Non-Governmental Organisation's (NGOs) Experiences*. Bangalore: HIVOS and NOVIB.

Rajasekhar, D. (1995). NGDOs, People and Decentralised Government in Karnataka. In D. Rajasekhar. *et al.* (eds.), *People Centred Rural Development: NGDOs and Decentralised Government*. Bangalore: ISEC, CDR, BCO and NOVIB.

Rajasekhar, D. (1997). Making the Community Banking Sustainable. *VOICES*, 1(2).

Rajasekhar, D. and Namerta (1994). Wage Labour in the Agricultural Sector. In Sarath Davala (ed.), *Unprotected Labour in India: Issues and Concerns*. New Delhi: FES.

Rajasekhar, D. and N.L. Narasimha Reddy (1997). *Local Development Programmes and NGOs: A Guide on Local Government Programmes for Field Workers*. Bangalore: BCO and NOVIB.

Reddy, N.L. Narasimha and D. Rajasekhar (1996). *Development Programmes and NGOs: A Guide on Central Government Programmes for NGOs in India*. Bangalore: BCO and NOVIB.

Robinson, M. (1993). Governance, Democracy and Conditionality: NGOs and the New Policy Agenda. In A. Clayton (ed.), *Governance, Democracy and Conditionality: What Role for NGOs?* Oxford: INTRAC.

5

NGO's ROLE IN INCREASING PEOPLE'S PARTICIPATION IN LOCAL DECENTRALISED GOVERNMENT

SUSANNE DAM HANSEN

INTRODUCTION

This paper examines the role of NGOs in facilitating linkages between their target group and the Decentralised Government, and the extent to which NGOs have helped the weaker sections of the population to gain more power within the structure of society. The case chosen for the study is PRIs, which came into existence in their current form with the Constitutional Amendment in 1993. With this amendment, the Indian Government has made an attempt to address the problems of lack of people's participation in development by, among other things, introducing a system of reservations for the marginalised sections such as the poor and women to enable them to enter into the decision-making bodies in rural areas. Although the importance of both decentralisation and people's participation has been recognised since independence, the tendencies of centralisation and concentration of power in the hands of traditionally stronger groups in rural areas continue. This is seen as an important reason for the lack of pro-poor rural development as the resources were cornered by the rural elite and the marginalised sections could neither change their situation nor gain any power.

The paper analyses the different approaches that the three selected NGOs from Karnataka have adopted to enable their target groups to participate better in the PRIs. The paper begins with a short conceptual background on decentralisation, followed by an introduction to the overall structure of PRIs and the possibilities that the marginalised sections have within this structure to gain power.

DECENTRALISATION AND PANCHAYAT RAJ

Decentralisation, democracy and people's participation in the political process are not new concepts in the development research—they have all been central to the debate on world development. The fact that decentralisation has not always improved the local delivery systems, wherever it has been implemented, does not seem to have deterred the proponents of decentralisation (Samoff 1990: 514). Many of them argue that the reasons for failure are wrong methods, high expectations and lack of space for decision-making at the local level. In the current development research, there are different approaches and decentralisation has been variously defined as decentration (spatial relocation of decision-making), delegation (assignment of specific decision-making authority), and devolution (transfer of responsibility for governance) (Samoff 1990: 515).

Much of the recent writings on decentralisation reflects an interventionist perspective under which the primary concern for some authors is administrative decentralisation. It is understood that, with administrative decentralisation, there will be a change from outside or from the Centre which will lead to an improvement in the implementation of development projects. Political aspects remain a secondary concern under this approach. The proximate politics of the attempt to decentralisation are important, though often they are not addressed systematically or critically. Success is to be measured by improved implementation of development schemes, not in concrete political mobilisation. Put somewhat differently, popular empowerment might be seen as generally desirable and perhaps a likely consequence of successful decentralised administration. At the same time, decentralised administration is understood to be desirable in its own terms with or without popular empowerment.

In contrast, for some authors, the primary concern is political decentralisation—the transfer of decision-making authority to previously under-represented or marginal groups. Their concern is not on the extent of administrative rearrangement; but, whether or not decision-making authority has actually been transferred; whether or not there has in fact been a decentralisation involving genuine devolution of power. In this approach, empowerment is central; and, if the institutional reforms do not empower the marginalised groups, then there is no real decentralisation at all. Since those in power tend to enhance, rather than reduce, their authority of power, they resist this genuine devolution of power. Hence, (real) decentralisation is certainly neither automatic nor inevitable consequence of organisational rearrangements. These authors, therefore, argue that administrative decentralisation is a facade for maintaining or reinforcing central authority and this is not a devolution of power at all (Samoff 1990: 516-7).

The focus in the two approaches differs on the devolution of power. While the administrative decentralisation approach claims that mere structural changes will lead to a higher degree of development, the political approach argues that mobilising of the people and devolution of power are necessary to obtain real decentralisation. This is not as simple as that, since implementation of decentralisation can also be a reinforcement of the state power at the local level by creating local power centres in the name of decentralisation. This means that a deeper analysis of power relations and the purpose and areas of decentralisation are necessary to understand to what extent decentralisation is possible or has taken place in a given context. This also means that there is no point in trying to construct a general strategy of decentralisation, since the extent of decentralisation that is desirable can be determined only in concrete situations. Similarly, the indicators and measures of attempts, and of the success of decentralisation are specific in particular situations and must refer both to goals to be achieved (not simply to the institutions created to achieve them) and to the transformation of power relations.

To understand the extent of the devolution of power and responsibility for development that has taken place in India, and more specifically in Karnataka, we have to examine the PRIs, and their goals regarding people's participation in the decision-making process and development in the rural areas.

PANCHAYAT RAJ INSTITUTIONS

Since independence there have been several attempts to obtain a higher degree of self-governance in rural areas. Several kinds of decentralisation have been central to this process, whether it was in the context of trying to make the community development programmes work, or of 'weight-shedding' work in the central bureaucracy, or of administrative efficiency, or indeed, of a strengthening party networks at the ground level. Decentralisation attempts have been evaluated by several committees, the most notable among them being the Balwantrai Mehta Committee (1954) and the Asoka Mehta Committee (1978). According to these committees, the decentralised structure in the form of a 'four pillar state', resting on the foundations of a four-fold sharing of power between the village, the district, state and the centre remained more in the realm of an idea than in practice. The following problems were highlighted by the evaluation committees as impediments for a successful decentralisation and devolution of power:

* The state and central governments were reluctant towards devolution of power to lower bodies.
* The implementation of decentralisation in the form of PRIs was the responsibility of the individual states and some of them failed to set up the PRIs or to conduct elections to the existing ones.
* In places where PRIs were constituted, they were found to be functioning in the grip of bureaucracy.
* The concentration of power with the big landlords and the upper castes in the rural areas.
* The limited powers assigned to the PRIs provide mandate only to look after developmental responsibilities.

The Central government wanted a better use of the resources, which was seen, by some authors, as the whole reason for providing

PRIs with limited mandate. Decentralisation attempts can, therefore, be seen as a way of making the administrative decision processes more effective without any real devolution of power. In this context, the Asoka Mehta Committee was also critical of the role of the bureaucracy. "The bureaucracy had probably its own role in dissociating the Panchayat Raj institutions from the development process. Several factors seem to have conditioned their perception. The system of line hierarchy would find favour with them as an organisational principle. The officers would feel that they are primarily accountable for results and financial proprieties to the state government. The officials knew no better than to trust their non-fraternity. They would, on the one hand, therefore, be averse to the Panchayat Raj institutions being entrusted with additional functions and on the other, would not easily get adjusted to working under the supervision of elected representatives".[1]

Based on the reports of the Balwantrai Mehta and the Asoka Mehta Committees, and steps taken towards decentralisation in the states of West Bengal and Karnataka in the late 1970s and the early 1980s, the discussion on PRIs and devolution of power to secure people's participation in the development process continued. This was further given importance in the late 1980s when the international agenda for development shifted from service delivery to aid based on people's involvement in their own development.

As a result of the debate on people's participation in their own development, new initiatives regarding PRIs were taken by the Central government and were 'formalised' in the 73rd Constitutional Amendment in 1993. Decentralisation, people's participation and democracy at the local level were given priority in the new political system in rural areas. The model adopted was a three-tier one with Zilla Panchayat at the district level, Taluk Panchayat Samithi at the taluk level and Gram Panchayat at the village level. Gram sabha consisting of all voters in a Gram Panchayat area is to be convened at least twice a year to incorporate their views into planning and implementation. The amendment made the following stringent rules to secure people's participation in PRIs:

* Elections at the village, taluk and district levels are to be held regularly, and at the village level they should be held on non-party lines.
* Seats are to be reserved for women and SC/ST in PRIs at different levels in accordance with the size of these groups in the population; and, at least, one-third of the seats should be occupied by women.
* Elections to PRIs, completing their five-year term, are mandatory.
* Constitution of a Finance Commission to review the finances every five years and to recommend the size of funds to be allocated to the Panchayats and also the principles and the basis on which taxes should be collected in a Panchayat area.
* It will be the responsibility of PRIs to implement government schemes and programmes aimed at economic development and social justice in rural areas.
* The responsibility of collecting taxes was also given to the PRIs (LRSC 1994).

By introducing the above, the Central government attempted to deal with the problems pointed out by the evaluation committees. Some states received the Constitutional Amendment with reluctance, while others with enthusiasm. Some states took up the task of organising elections soon after the legislation, whereas a few states did not hold the mandatory elections until 1996 despite pressure from both the High and Supreme Courts.

PRIs IN KARNATAKA

The Karnataka Panchayat Raj Act of 1985 attracted nationwide attention because of its radical provisions on devolution of powers to the districts and villages (Mathew 1994: 50). The Act was based on the recommendations of the Asoka Mehta Committee and had a two-tier system with direct elections. The Act was made further radical by introducing reservations for women and SC/

ST to ensure the participation of the marginalised sections. Elections were held in 1987 and this model of PRIs was carried out in Karnataka until the Central government made the 73rd Constitutional Amendment. In accordance with the Amendment, Karnataka was forced to replace the 1985 Act and the elections at the village level were held in 1994.

The 73rd Amendment was radical in nature; but how much change did PRIs really bring in rural areas regarding people's participation and people-centered rural development? This question becomes important because, as pointed out in the discussion on decentralisation, the structural changes may not lead to a higher degree of development and people's participation merely by organisational rearrangements. Structures cannot act which means it becomes important to look at power relations and the actors' ability to act within the structure.

THE ACTORS WITHIN THE STRUCTURE

The aim of decentralisation and devolution of powers to the local government institutions was to secure the participation of the people in rural areas. But, as pointed out by the previous evaluation committees, there was a tendency towards concentration of power in the traditionally stronger groups such as landlords and upper castes. To overcome this problem, the 73rd Constitutional Amendment introduced a reservation policy to secure participation of the marginalised sections in the society.

The marginalised sections such as women, SCs and STs in India are characterised by economic, social and political backwardness and have not been involved in public life and decision-making processes. This reservation policy was questioned on the grounds that structural changes in the form of reservation cannot break the traditional patterns and bring awareness and power to the people overnight.

In this context, it becomes relevant to look at other actors within the structure who could enhance the process of securing the participation of the weaker sections not only on paper, but also in reality. The NGOs are the other important actors working with the marginalised sections in the rural areas of Karnataka.

During 1980s, many of these NGOs, in accordance with the international development environment, shifted from an aid approach based on service delivery to a more people-centred development approach and had taken up issues such as women and poor people's empowerment as their new working agenda (Rajasekhar 1997).

This shift in the international development environment emerged out of a recognition that mere service delivery does not enhance sustainable development. Several decades of development has shown that without people's participation not only in the development process, but also in the institutions which determine the development, a change and improvement in the standard of living of the people were difficult to be obtained. This means that people-centered development has to be seen in coherence with decentralisation and devolution of power as the former is linked to the latter. "Arguments for decentralisation of government usually proceed along the lines that decentralised local government institutions make the state more participatory, thereby more accountable, and thereby more efficient. The rural poor majority can assert their interests, and the local government institutions and the development they undertake begins to be more sustainable" (Webster 1995: 21).

Together with a change in the international agenda towards a more people-centered development, there has also been a change in the way local government institutions and local NGOs are viewed. Previously, the dominant tendency was to view the NGOs and the local government as competitors either from a perspective based upon the assessment of their organisational efficiency and effectiveness or from a more ideological standpoint based on the rejection of the state's role in development. Today, there is a strong opinion that a comparison of the functional strengths and weaknesses of the different organisations can lead to the identification of a complementary approach in rural development (Webster 1995).

In the light of the changes in the development agenda and the implementation of decentralisation, new roles for the NGOs have emerged as facilitators at the local level between the weaker sections and the state. Some of the advantages seen to be possessed by the local NGOs are that they are potentially more actor-oriented because "they represent local interests; they are more flexible in their methods and practices because they tend to be local and relatively small; they are more participatory in their organisation not least because they are less hierarchical; they are more focused in their development work as it is their principal goal; they are more independent from local power structures and local political elites; and finally, they are more effective as they can better target their intervention" (Webster 1995: 26).

The role of the NGOs is not just limited to being facilitators at the local level. Due to the qualities that NGOs are seen to possess, they can also, as institutions within society, take up initiatives to change the structure by organising networks both at the micro-and-macro levels and put pressure on the government; they can lobby on behalf of the weaker sections and can seek to enable their target groups to participate in the decision-making process regarding their own development. This means that the role of the NGOs in a decentralised structure is not merely limited to doing development better but also they can create a link with the government institutions as facilitators and at the same time undertake advocacy to the benefit of the weaker sections at both micro-and-macro levels.

NGOs IN KARNATAKA

The 73rd Constitutional Amendment gave the possibility for the NGOs to play a role as facilitators between the weaker sections and the decentralised government institutions as they were already working with these groups. Further, elections to Gram Panchayats on non-party basis provided, in theory, some space for the NGOs to become involved in PRIs as the NGOs could retain their apolitical status[2]. The NGOs in Karnataka were dubious towards the new decentralised political structure in the beginning, as some of them saw the PRIs as just another cosmetic attempt in the name of democracy and participation. In spite of this, the NGOs were, to some extent, forced to redefine their roles for the following reasons:

* The PRIs have become part of the structure within which the NGOs have to work in the rural areas.
* The target group of many of the NGOs have become Gram Panchayat members largely because of reservations for the marginalised groups.
* Structural changes in PRIs are aimed at people-centered rural development, which is also the objective of many of the NGOs.
* Many donor agencies have changed their development agenda towards empowerment of the poor so that they themselves can take action and change their own situation. This means that project funds are given to programmes which aim at enabling the weaker sections to gain access to the political processes which influence the society in which they live.

In response to these factors, some NGOs gradually changed their attitude to PRIs as the time for elections at the village level approached in 1993. This process was further strengthened by the debate which took place in both media and the academic world regarding the possibilities of people-centered rural development with PRIs. One of the themes of this debate was the earlier mentioned concern about whether the weaker sections would be able to perform in office or the earlier experiences of concentration of power with the traditional stronger groups would take place again.

A need for training not only for the people who would be elected, but also for the voters emerged out of this debate. In this context, many international donor agencies approached the government with funds to train the weaker sections of the population to perform in the decentralised government institutions as participation of the weaker sections in the decision-making process was in line with the international donor policy of people's empowerment.

Due to the advantages seen to be possessed by the NGOs in their more local approach and their advantage of being more independent of local power and political elites, the Government of Karnataka asked several resource NGOs to undertake the task of training these weaker sections. Besides that, the government also sent out an appeal to the local NGOs working in the rural areas that they should integrate awareness on the local government institutions in their working approach and if possible also take up the task of training the Gram Panchayat members as a separate programme. The government did this in the realisation that it would be impossible for the government to reach the 80,627 Gram Panchayat members within the state, and even if the government only aimed at the members elected on reserved seats the task would still be impossible. In addition to this, the government felt that the NGOs have an advantage in reaching the members at the village level as they were known in the area, they spoke the local language and were familiar with the local conditions whereas the training for the two higher levels (taluk and district) of the PRIs was more accessible for outsiders[3].

Many of the training programmes taken up by the resource NGOs after the Gram Panchayat elections were for women, since it was felt that this social group, excluded from the public life, for cultural and traditional reasons, were the most important group to address if the reservation policy should have any success. A study carried out in Karnataka regarding women's new role in PRIs characterised the new situation as follows: "The policy of reservation for women adopted by the Indian government has offered them an important opportunity, to be more significant actors in the political process. However, it remains the case that these Gram Panchayat members are new in positions of power, and authority and the question of providing some form of external support is, therefore, crucial" (Anitha and Gayathri 1995: 91).

Depending on their individual working strategy, the NGOs in the rural areas in Karnataka undertook different positions on their involvement in PRIs (Rajasekhar 1995). Some decided that they would stay out of it and leave it to the target group members as to whether they should participate in the elections or not.

Others integrated the PRIs in their working agenda and used all their means to get somebody from their target group elected. The main obstacle for many NGOs was that they did not want to get involved in politics as they feared divisions within the target group organisations at the village level. As to the question of taking up the task of training, many of them were unsure among themselves about what this new decentralised structure would bring along. Another factor was that the NGOs were reluctant to move outside their target group and provide training for all the Gram Panchayat members as that might cause problems to the development work based on target group approach.

DIFFERENT NGO APPROACHES TO PRIs: THE CASE OF THREE NGOs FROM KARNATAKA

In order to observe the impact of the different NGO approaches towards PRIs, three NGOs from Karnataka were selected. The identity of NGOs is concealed by calling them as NGO A, B and C. The methodology adopted was to look at Gram Panchayats in three villages in each of the NGO project areas. The villages were selected with the help of the NGOs, on the criteria of similarity in size and in socio-economic status. Another criteria was the degree of interaction between the village and the NGO to see whether this has made any difference in the functioning of the Gram Panchayat members from the weaker sections. The different degrees of interaction between the villages and the NGOs are as follows: (1) A high degree of interaction with the NGO; (2) less interaction; and (3) no interaction. Members from nine Gram Panchayats in the three NGO project[4] areas who were elected on reserved seats, were interviewed.

NGO-A

NGO-A was started in 1984, and has been involved in organising Dalit Sanghas in 150 villages spread over four different taluks in Tumkur district. The short term goal of the NGO is to look into the ways and means of increasing the socio-economic, political and cultural bargaining power of the Dalits in the district. The

NGO believes that the achievement of this will be the consequence of not only a critical consciousness among Dalits, but also the will to articulate and decide to use these powers in a way that will lead them to their own development. This goal is translated into action by starting Sanghas making use of adult education and Balwadis as entry points among men and women respectively. Besides the Sanghas, the NGO is running four-month training programmes for young Dalits selected from each village with the aim that awareness on Dalit's rights and culture is provided and potential leaders for a Dalit movement produced. The NGO believes that the only way of changing the situation of Dalits in the society is by mobilising young people in larger numbers so that they initiate and sustain a Dalit movement. This is done by organising the Dalits not only in Sanghas, but also in taluk and district committees. In relation to the PRIs, the NGO was involved in giving pre-election awareness to its target group in the form of handing out pamphlets in the local language. The pamphlets gave an orientation on the PRI and the importance of voting for a good candidate with the right qualities. After the elections, the NGO did not provide training to the elected members from the target group as a resource NGO from Bangalore provided training for the elected women Gram Panchayat members in the area and the NGO felt that there was no need to duplicate the work.

NGO-B

NGO-B was set up in 1979-80 as a facilitating organisation for small groups in Karnataka and Tamil Nadu, but it began to concentrate its work in Bangalore rural district in 1984-85. The programme emphasises on awareness creation and organisation of landless labourers and poor farmers across caste lines into Sanghas and associations. Later, basic health, training for women's development, children's education, environmental regeneration, agriculture, saving and credit, housing campaign and networking were integrated into the work. The NGO is, at present, working in 150 villages spread over three different taluks and have 38 staff members. The short term goals of the NGO are to give awareness training to the poor and build up Sanghas of the poor in all the villages. These Sanghas will function as forums for training and general awareness building and are coordinated at the taluk level.

Regarding PRIs, the NGO gave general awareness training in its Sangha meetings and also conducted one day training on the structure of the PRI to all its target group members before Gram Panchayat elections. The NGO emphasised the importance of getting some one from the target group elected, but left the choice of the candidate to the Sangha itself. After the election, no training programme was conducted for the elected members, but the NGO is planning to give training to the members elected from the target group.

NGO-C

NGO-C was started in 1977 in Kolar district and is, at present, working in 457 villages spread out in three taluks (in 1995 the NGO withdrew from the taluk where they originally started). The NGO had, in 1994, 128 full-time staff members, but the number has been reduced slowly during 1995 in accordance with their withdrawal from one taluk. The main objective of the NGO is to organise coolie[5] workers in Sanghas across caste lines and to build up taluk level mass organisations, so that coolies struggling for their development can continually cope with wider societal changes. The NGO is also working against gender discrimination and has taken up dry-land development programmes and credit funds to improve the economic situation of the coolie families.

The NGO has a history of pursuing a highly political approach and the target group has previously taken part in the Mandal Panchayat election and has taken up many controversial issues along the way. Among the Sanghas, there is a very high pro-Sangha feeling and they regard themselves as an island within the village. This feeling is part of the NGO strategy, since a very strict discipline is kept regarding meetings and procedures, which includes that meetings are held every week in spite of harvest work, for example, and minutes are written on almost every meeting. Besides the Sangha meetings, the women from the Sangha have a meeting once a week where they discuss the budget of the health programme and problems related to women. They also discuss loan applications for the coolie credit fund, since the women are given sanction power to see that their husbands do not take loans without an agreement of their wives. Due to their previous experience with the election for the Mandal Panchayats which caused a lot of problem among the coolies the NGO was a bit reluctant to take part in the elections for the Gram Panchayats. As election time approached, the coolie organisation decided to take part and the NGO gave the Sanghas support in making election strategies for the candidates from the target group and alliances with other groups within the village. After the election, the NGO staff followed up the work of the Gram Panchayat members elected from among the target group, but no actual training has been given by the NGO. Training from outside has been provided to all the Gram Panchayat members in two phases with foreign funding.

The presentation of the NGOs and the overall scheme (Chart 5.1) shows that the NGOs took different approaches towards the Gram Panchayat elections and that the training given from outside also differed among the three project areas.

PARAMETERS FOR THE FIELDWORK

Several parameters have been used to highlight the impact of the NGO approach and the training to see whether the intervention of the NGOs made any difference in the participation of the target group in the elections and in their work as Gram Panchayat members. This has been seen in relation to the Gram Panchayat members from the weaker sections outside the target group by interviewing elected members from one control village adjacent to each NGO project area.

Pre-election approach and participation of target group

The different pre-election approaches taken by the NGOs made a difference in the participation of the target group in various ways. NGO-C had the highest participation of the Sangha as a

CHART 5.1: THE DIFFERENT APPROACHES TO PRIs BY THE SELECTED NGO

Particulars	*NGO-A*	*NGO-B*	*NGO-C*
Target group	Dalits	Landless labour and poor farmers across caste lines.	Coolies across caste lines.
Working areas	Organising Sanghas and building up a Dalit movement.	Organising Sanghas and providing general awareness.	Organising Sanghas and coolie organisation.
No. of villages	150	150	457
No. of full-time staff	Approx. 20	Approx. 38	Approx. 100
Pre-election approach	The NGO handed out pamphlets regarding the PRIs and what qualities to look for in the candidate when the target group members are voting.	The NGO explained about the PRI in their Sangha meetings and encouraged their target group to choose someone among themselves to stand for election.	The NGO supported their target group by helping them in making election strategies and alliances with other groups in the village.
Post-election training	Four-day training was conducted for all the women Gram Panchayat members in two phases.	No training was given, but the NGO is planning to provide training for the Gram Panchayat members from their target group.	Four-day training was conducted for both women and men in two phases. One phase strictly for women and another for both women and men.

whole, as it was deeply involved in getting a candidate among themselves elected. This had the consequence that the work of the Gram Panchayat member after the election was followed closely by the Sangha and there was a communication link between the local government institutions and Sangha members.

NGO-B maintained a low profile in the Gram Panchayat elections as several problems arose during and after the elections. First of all, the Sanghas were unable to agree on a single candidate among the Sangha members and had not been involved as a unit to make alliances and get one person elected. In one of the

Sanghas, this lack of unity resulted in a Sangha member winning the election with support from the higher castes in the village and leaving the Sangha soon after the election. In another case, a candidate had won with only a difference of three votes from the other candidate in the Sangha and many felt that the other candidate was the most suitable. This lack of unity during the pre-election period showed lack of accountability towards the Sangha, as there was not the same degree of communication link between the Sangha and the Gram Panchayat member in the form of discussions at the Sangha meetings as in the case of NGO-C.

The NGO-A did not play an active role either in the pre-election period or afterwards. The Sanghas had only in one of the villages got their own candidate elected. But this woman had very little knowledge of the responsibilities and functioning of the Gram Panchayat and did not inform the Sangha about what was going on in the Gram Panchayat meetings. Further, the Sangha did not ask her either, so no communication link was created. In another case, a Dalit woman was elected, but she did not represent the Dalits as such, as she was socially and economically better off. The NGO had worked in this village for four years, but after it had withdrawn the Sangha had to be dissolved and in spite of four years of NGO work no member from the previous target group had stood for the election.

Women's participation

The participation of the women Gram Panchayat members from the target group also differed. The approach of NGO-C to conduct separate women meetings made women very active in both the Sangha and Gram Panchayats. A woman President, in spite of being illiterate and landless, had great knowledge of the responsibility and functioning of the Gram Panchayat. She claimed that she gained her skills by being a Sangha member and she had learned to address problems and speak in bigger forums on the importance of women taking part in the public life. She also said that the staff from the NGO helped her to get elected and stories of how she went into exile before election because she was afraid of getting kidnapped by the groups who supported another candidate were narrated.

In the cases of NGO-A and NGO-B, the participation of women in Gram Panchayats was less visible. One elected woman from the target group of NGO-A knew very little about the responsibilities and functioning of the Gram Panchayat and stated that the meetings were dominated by high caste members and matters regarding funds were only known to the President of the Gram Panchayat. Another Dalit woman, who was also a President of the Gram Panchayat in her area, had a great knowledge of the functioning and responsibilities of the Gram Panchayat, but as she was socially and economically better off than the rest in the Dalit colony, she did not really represent the target group of the NGO.

A woman elected member from the target group of NGO-B has, as mentioned earlier, left the Sangha after elections. The Sangha claimed that she has been taking care of only her own interests, which could be seen in the way that the drainage sanctioned to the village was implemented outside her own house in spite of the fact that this was not a priority area. The woman member herself stated that she stood for the election because her family traditionally participated in the old Panchayat system. Her decision to contest was also because of the reservation for women and the encouragement provided by the high castes. She did not know much about the responsibilities of the Gram Panchayat as such and had no knowledge of the schemes or funds available for the Gram Panchayats.

Post-election training

Different forms of post-election training from outside were conducted in different areas of the NGOs except in the case of NGO-B where no training was organised at all.

In the project area of NGO-A, a resource NGO (SEARCH) from Bangalore conducted training for local trainers who afterwards conducted a two-phase training programme in the local area. The training was strictly for women and was offered to all the female Gram Panchayat members. However, not all of them attended because it was hard to leave their work and home for several days, as the training was done in two phases of four days duration. Other reasons for their absence were that their husbands would not let them go or they did not simply prioritise the training due to domestic responsibilities.

The women members, who did attend the training programme, expressed their satisfaction regarding the training and said that they had learned about the role of women in politics, about responsibility, and about the functioning of the Gram Panchayats. They were also happy with the way the training was conducted, since a variety of learning methods involving audio visual equipment, games and drama were used. In addition, the resource NGO had developed some materials which were given to the members as reference books later on. The books were user-friendly with drawings, and were written in simple local language.

In the case of NGO-B, no outside institution gave any training in the area, but the NGO was planning to call all their elected target group members together for training. So far, they have only called for one discussion meeting at which not many turned up due to the harvest season. Accordingly, the impact of the NGO's efforts in this area has yet to be seen. However, in this area the Government of Karnataka provided all the Gram Panchayat members with a book on the functioning and responsibilities of the Gram Panchayat when the members attended their first meeting. The books, however, were of very little use to the people who were illiterate, as there were no illustrations or drawings they could relate to.

In the case of NGO-C, the training programme conducted to all the Gram Panchayat members in the project area with foreign funding, had taken place in two phases. The first phase was exclusively for women and issues related to their new political role in Gram Panchayats. During the second phase, which was for both men and women, information on the functioning and responsibilities of the Gram Panchayats was passed on to the members. A book was distributed to the members during the training which gave information on the functioning of the Gram

Panchayats. This book, using drawings and simple language, was user-friendly towards people who could not read.

All the Gram Panchayat members from NGO-C, who underwent training, felt that it had been useful in their work as Gram Panchayat members. The elected members said that they had little knowledge of the responsibilities and functioning of the Gram Panchayats when they first got elected. They stated that, through the training, they learned quite a few aspects and now they are able to perform better. Some of them expressed that further training on drainage, sanitation and so on could help them improve the standard of living in the villages with relatively small size of funds.

Different levels of NGO interaction

Due to the different roles that the NGO have played regarding PRIs, the differences between villages with high, low or no interaction could best be seen in the villages visited in the areas of NGO-B and NGO-C.

In the village where NGO-B was not working, there was supposed to be a Dalit woman elected. I was met by another Gram Panchayat member who was elected on a general seat from the same village. He told me that the woman elected on the reserved seat had gone to live with her son in the nearest town and that he was taking care of everything. The elected woman member only had to come for the Gram Panchayat meetings and sign the way he told her.

Between the high and low interaction villages of NGO-B, the Sangha was clearly stronger in the village where the NGO had worked for a long time, which could be seen in the way they discussed and also towards their criticism of the Gram Panchayat member who had left the Sangha after the election. The latter showed that they were aware of the responsibilities of their Gram Panchayat member as they were criticising her for not performing for the benefit of the village.

In the village which had low interaction with NGO-B, the Sangha was not as well established. The members were not as critical as in the previous village and the Sangha meetings were basically consisted of discussion on how to make the credit and saving programme run. The Sangha forum was not used for the discussion of political issues and no practice of giving information by the Gram Panchayat member was implemented in the meeting agenda which meant that communication between the decentralised government institutions and the Sangha did not take place as the member claimed that no one asked him either.

In the case of NGO-C, the interaction level could clearly be seen as the members from the villages where the NGO had worked for a long time were very much aware of the political situation. The work of the Gram Panchayat member was closely monitored by the other Sangha members. In the village where the NGO was not working one ST woman was elected because her cousin was a rich ST in the village and he had wanted to stand for election, but could not because of the reservations. The woman herself had no knowledge of the functioning of the Gram Panchayat and told that she only went to sign and that she did what she was told by her male relative. There was no interest in the Gram Panchayat from the village as such, as local power dynamics were ruling the scene.

The link between the elected members from the target group and the rest of the villages

As the Gram Panchayat members in principle represent the interests of the village as a whole within the local government institutions there should be some form of information linkage between these bodies and the villages through the Gram Panchayat member. According to the Panchayat Act, this linkage should be created by conducting Gram Sabha meetings every six months, in which the whole village would assemble and discuss the problems that needed to be addressed and receive feedback from the Gram Panchayat members about the work and functioning of the local government institutions. Unfortunately, this does not happen very often in practice. Only few of the Gram Panchayat members said that they had called for Gram sabha meetings and discussed with the rest of the village and provided information on the work of the Gram Panchayats. The other members were either not aware of this requirement or else said that it was difficult to bring the whole village together as there were so many clashes of interest within the village.

Another forum for discussion and feedback is in the Sangha with members elected to the Gram Panchayat. This forum is in nature easier to access as it is smaller, the members know each other, they meet regularly on other issues and the women here play an equal role as members.

In the case of NGO-C this forum was very much used to create a link with the local government institutions. Here, there was a tradition of political involvement and the elections had been a major issue at the meetings. In the cases of NGO-A and NGO-B, this forum was not used to the same extent and the accountability towards the Sangha was not as high as in the case of NGO-C. The Sanghas from NGO-A and NGO-B did not possess the same sense of unity and had not been active in getting their own members elected for the local government institutions.

General problems in the functioning of the Gram Panchayats

One of the problems that all the Gram Panchayat members mentioned was the lack of funds, as the final budget for PRIs is not yet decided by the Finance Commission at the state level. This means that the Gram Panchayats are left with an average amount of Rs. 1.25 lakh per year which is allocated from the state along with different development programmes. In addition, the individual Gram Panchayats could collect taxes in the local area. But, due to limited sources of tax in the rural areas and the general resistance to pay these taxes, this does not give the Gram Panchayats much income.

As a result, many Gram Panchayat members felt that it was difficult to do anything except wait for the schemes to get sanctioned from the higher levels. In this context, a woman member from NGO-A said that in spite of the reservation of seats for ST/SC, high caste members still constitute a majority in the Gram Panchayats which meant that the schemes and money often went to their parts of the village, to their relatives or to their supporters amongst the lowest castes. Problems relating to party politics were also mentioned during the fieldwork despite that elections to the Gram Panchayats were supposed to be held on non-party lines. Several members said that there was a tendency at the higher levels (taluk and district) to favour the Gram Panchayat with the same political majority as themselves.

CONCLUSIONS

The paper began by arguing that structural changes do not necessarily lead to a higher participation of the people, as structures cannot act and there is a need to look at the actors within the structure. Further, structural changes in the form of reservation policy do not lead to automatic participation of the intended groups, as it takes a long time to break the traditional patterns, and further structural changes in the form of land reforms, land rights for women and so forth are necessary to achieve the intended goal.

The paper chose to look at the decentralised structure as it is implemented in Karnataka and took a closer look at the actors within the structure. As one of the objectives with decentralisation was to secure the participation of the weaker sections in the local government institutions and as this group traditionally have been marginalised in the society, the paper focused on the NGO as another actor which could enhance the process of the participation of the weaker sections.

The paper showed that the role of the NGO did make a difference in some areas and that the NGOs in the future can play roles as advocates at both micro- and macro- levels which could lead to better participation and functioning of the weaker sections in the decentralised government institutions.

The role of the NGO was most visible in the case of NGO-C which has a political approach and which has been involved in the previous Mandal Panchayat elections in Karnataka. The Gram Panchayat members from the target group stated that though they had learned the responsibilities and functioning of the Gram Panchayat from the training conducted from outside, the experience and skills in analysing and addressing the problems at the village level were obtained as Sangha members. Especially, one woman member felt that her experience as a Sangha member had helped her in the new role as a Gram Panchayat member. As Sangha member, she learned the important role that women can play and also how to speak in bigger forums which were traditionally dominated by men in the village.

The target group of NGO-C was very much aware of the functioning and responsibilities of the decentralised government institutions and the Sanghas were used as a forum of discussion and information on the work of the Gram Panchayats. One can say that a communication link and participation have been created between the Sangha and the local government institutions. The link between Sangha and the local government institutions is a positive sign of people's participation. But, one must also be aware of the danger in this as the Sangha does not represent all the people from the weaker sections and there is a danger of exclusion if the Gram Panchayat members do not develop an accountability not only towards the Sangha, but also to the rest of the village. There are, of course, other Gram Panchayat members from outside the target group who also represent the village; but, the history of the PRIs has shown that there is a tendency to neglect the interests of the weaker sections. Therefore, it is important that the mandatory Gram Sabha meetings are held and that the decisions on development work in the villages discussed in the village as a whole, so that the communication link between the village and the decentralised government institutions is not limited to sub-groups in the village.

This applies for NGO-A and NGO-B as well, even though the Sangha meetings were not used for discussions to the same extent as in the case of NGO-C. In this context, the NGOs have a role to play in encouraging their target group members to discuss the work of the Gram Panchayats in a wider context and ask their Gram Panchayat members for information on the work of the Gram Panchayats. This applies to all the Sanghas with or without a member from their own group in the local government institutions. It is important that the weaker sections ask for accountability of elected leaders, as one of the purposes of decentralisation is that the weaker sections can assert their interests through their local elected members and take part in the decision-making process.

The paper also showed that the NGOs can play a role by incorporating the decentralised government institutions in their working approach and by giving information on the PRIs, giving support to their women members in the form of skill building and confidence, by giving support during the elections, and also to the elected members as this helps the members to perform better in their new office. In addition, it is important that the NGOs encourage their target group members to discuss political issues and support them in using the possibilities that the decentralised structure has created. These things put pressure on the NGOs to move away from their traditionally non-political approach and the tendency to work with only one group of people in a village.

It is important that the NGOs take up the task of training the elected members not only from their target group, but all the elected members in the project area in a separate programme as the government itself realised that it cannot do that. Most of the NGOs have good knowledge of local culture and conditions and they should seek to use this to enable not only their target group but the village as a whole to once again turn their attention towards the state and the structure within the society, because only with accountability from the state and people's own participation can development take place. NGOs, as other actors within the structure, should seek to enable the people to change and use the democratic structure within which they live. The NGO role is not just limited to that of facilitator at the micro-level. By organising networks at both micro- and macro- levels, they could also advocate for more funds to the PRIs, better technical support to the development work in the village and organise training and share information among the different NGOs.

NOTES

1. Cited in Mathew (1994: 12-3).
2. NGOs in India have had a long tradition of not getting involved in party politics. This was a legal requirement. In addition, the international donor

environment has had a policy of avoiding involvement in party politics. All this meant that development work was essentially service delivery rather than focusing on structural changes.

3. Personal communication from the Director, Ministry of Rural Development and Panchayat Raj, Bangalore, Karnataka.
4. Before the data are presented, one limitation has to be mentioned as it may have a bearing on the conclusions. Though elections to Gram Panchayats took place in December 1993, most of the training programmes were just concluded by the time the fieldwork was taken up in autumn 1995. This means that it is early to assess the impact of training on the participation of women as Gram Panchayat members.
5. This NGO defines a coolie (literal meaning labourer) as one who does not employ labourers. This implies that coolies belong to landed and landless agricultural labour families who do not employ wage labourers for their own lands: but depend on mutual exchange labour practices for cultivating their lands.

REFERENCES

Anitha, B.K. and V. Gayathri (1995). Training Initiatives for Gram Panchayat Members in Karnataka. In D. Rajasekhar *et al.* (eds.), *People-centered Rural Development: NGDOs and Decentralised Government*. Bangalore: ISEC, CDR, BCO and NOVIB.

Aziz, Abdul (1993). *Decentralised Planning: The Karnataka Experiment*. New Delhi: SAGE.

Government of Karnataka (1993). *The Karnataka Panchayat Raj Act, 1993*. Bangalore: Law & Parliamentary Affairs, Government of Karnataka.

LRSC (1994). *Legal Perspectives*. Documentation File No. 32. Chingelpet: Legal Resources for Social Action.

Mathew, George (1994). *Panchayati Raj - From Legislation to Movement*. New Delhi: Concept.

Rajasekhar, D. (1995). NGDOs, People and Decentralised Government in Karnataka. In D Rajasekhar *et al.* (eds.), *People-centered Rural Development: NGDOs and Decentralised Government*. Bangalore: ISEC, CDR, BCO and NOVIB.

Rajasekhar, D. (1997). Rural Development Strategies of NGOs. *Journal of Social and Economic Development*, 1 (2).

Samoff, Joel (1990). Decentralisation: The Politics of Interventionism. *Development and Change*, 21 (3):

Webster, Neil (1995). A Conceptual Approach to NGDOs and Panchayat Raj in Rural Development. In D. Rajasekhar *et al.* (eds.), *People-centered Rural Development: NGDOs and Decentralised Government*. Bangalore: ISEC, CDR, BCO and NOVIB.

6

EMPOWERMENT OF GRAM PANCHAYAT MEMBERS: EXPERIENCES OF YOUNG INDIA PROJECT, PENUKONDA, ANDHRA PRADESH

G. SUVARCHALA

INTRODUCTION

Of late, the policy makers and political party leaders across the country have been making efforts to widen the political power base so as to ensure the participation of hitherto marginalised sections—women, backwards and scheduled castes and tribes—in the political processes at micro-, meso- and macro-levels. The political power base of the marginalised sections is proposed to be widened by providing opportunities in the form of reserving certain percentage of seats in the PRIs, Legislative Assembly and the Parliament. While the process at the micro-level was completed and elections conducted, efforts to broad-base the political power of the marginalised sections is still an ongoing process at the meso- and macro-levels.

At the micro-level, opportunities have been provided for women and backward castes in the PRIs under the 73rd Constitutional Amendment by reserving 33 per cent of the total ward membership and executive positions available. This is, in addition to the existing reservation of 15 per cent and 3 per cent of the total seats for scheduled castes and tribes, respectively. Further, the Amendment has not only accorded constitutional status to Panchayats but also widened their developmental role by extending a higher degree of delegation of powers. This, in a way, has also provided greater opportunities for an active participation of NGOs *vis-a-vis* the Gram Panchayats and decentralised governance.

The concepts of decentralised governance and PRIs are, however, not new to the NGOs, be it in Andhra Pradesh or elsewhere, especially for those working at the grassroots level. Most of the NGOs, working at the grassroots level, in the course of implementing their programmes, interact with the Panchayat members as a matter of course. What is, however, new is the changing approach and vision of NGOs towards developmental problems of the people, decentralised governance and Panchayats. Encouraging and enabling people to acquire control over structures vested with resources and their distribution has been gaining currency among the NGOs. This process has been further catalysed by the constitutional amendment and the elections that followed by its ratification.

In the light of the provisions of the Amendment, many NGOs assumed an active role in encouraging their target groups to utilise the new opportunities and contest the elections to Gram Panchayats. Among the NGOs working in Andhra Pradesh, Young India Project (YIP) utilised the new opportunities successfully and achieved spectacular results. Its target group members secured positions either at the ward level or at the executive level or at both levels in more than 500 Gram Panchayats spread over six districts (Anantapur, Cuddapah, Chittoor, Nellore, Kurnool and Nalgonda) of Andhra Pradesh. Given the spectacular electoral performance of YIP's target group members in Gram Panchayats, an attempt has been made here to share the experience of YIP as this would provide useful lessons to other NGOs. This would also provide pointers about the degree of empowerment that the political reservations can confer, the extent of participation of newly elected members, and the limitations that the NGOs may confront in the process. The term empowerment is used here in a broader sense of both capturing power positions and ability to take independent and just decisions to ensure the proper distribution of resources.

The issue of empowerment in the present paper is analysed using a part of information collected for a study[1] on interaction of agricultural labour unions with Gram Panchayats. The information was collected through interviews and group discussions with the staff of YIP at various levels, starting from Mandal to project level and union and Gram Panchayat members and office bearers.

BACKGROUND OF YIP

The background information presented here includes objectives, approach, strategy, activities and organisational set-up of the YIP. YIP has been striving to alleviate poverty and improve the living standards of agricultural and non-agricultural labourers, marginal and small farmers irrespective of their caste background for the past twenty years. Initially, it started the work in Anantapur district and extended the area of operation to five other districts, namely, Chittoor, Nellore, Kurnool, Cuddapah and Nalgonda. Currently, it is operating in 240 mandals spread over these districts.

In order to realise the set objectives, YIP adopted an organisational-mobilisational approach and formed agricultural labour unions. The unions formed at the village level are federated at the mandal and district levels. The unions at different levels have an executive committee consisting of a president, secretary and a few members. The president and the secretary organise periodic meetings of the unions to discuss the ongoing activities. It is through the unions that the target community is provided assistance for various economic activities: amenities like ration cards, house site *pattas* and land acquisition under the land reform legislations by organising the struggles. Further, to ensure the smooth flow and just distribution of resources, YIP has also encouraged the union members to contest and gain access to political positions at the Gram Panchayat level. The economic/ development programmes of Central and state governments and the reservation in Panchayats are used by the YIP essentially to strengthen the unions and the process of unionisation.

The organisational set-up of the YIP is such that it has a president and secretary at the project level, district coordinator/

secretary at the district level, group leader for a cluster of Mandals and a Mandal coordinator/secretary at the Mandal level. It is the Mandal coordinator/secretary who maintains regular contact with the representatives of union members and villagers; organises periodic meetings of the unions, and is in-charge of all the activities undertaken at the Mandal level.

Pre-election strategy

Keeping its own objectives in view, the YIP has utilised the opportunity provided by the 73rd Amendment and encouraged the union members to contest the Panchayat elections. YIP supported the members at the Gram Panchayat level where elections were held on the basis of non-political party symbols. It, however, has not discouraged any of the members to contest the Mandal and Zilla Praja parishad elections. It may be noted here that as the elections at the Mandal and district levels were held on political party basis, the YIP wanted to keep away from party politics, and hence, restrained from entering into alliances with any of the political parties.

In order to ensure the success of the union members, the YIP adopted a three-pronged strategy. Firstly, it provided pre-election awareness to all the members. The pre-election awareness comprises of issues like importance of utilising the 33 per cent reservations, voting rights, information on rigging, booth capturing and other malpractices normally followed during the elections. Precautions and steps to be followed in preventing the occurrence of such malpractices are also discussed. Secondly, unions were encouraged to organise meetings to select the candidates. The selection process was entirely left to the members and, at no point, did the staff intervene to influence the decisions of the unions. In the event of lack of consensus, the YIP had allowed more than one candidate to contest for the same seat. The requisite deposit and election expenses were borne by the candidates themselves. Thirdly, in order to ensure the success of the candidates from the unions, the YIP entered into a strategic alliance with non-union members from backward and scheduled castes and tribes such that mutual support was extended by each other.

The three pronged strategy adopted by the YIP enabled the union members to win 5,620 Ward member seats and 511 Sarpanch seats in 124 Mandals in its project area. Table 6.1 provides details about the electoral successes of union members including physically disabled across the project districts. Further, as a result of reservation and the above strategy, for the first time, scheduled/ backward caste women belonging to the unions managed to gain control over the post of Sarpanch. In some Panchayats, the representation of women at the membership level accounted for four to five out of a total of nine to ten seats.

Notwithstanding the efforts of the YIP to utilise the new opportunities and the electoral successes of its union members, what is, however, important is to analyse the extent to which the reservations enabled the marginalised sections to enter into Gram Panchayats; how effective is their participation and thus the functioning of Gram Panchayat in ensuring the smooth flow and just distribution of resources; and the limitations experienced by the NGO in the process. To understand this process, an attempt has been made here to present the case studies of three union member dominated Gram Panchayats by using the information on composition, profile of members and activities taken up. While doing so, attention has been focused mainly on ward members from the unions.

The selected three Gram Panchayats are Gummagatta, Pandiparti and Naginayini Cheruvu. In the case of Pandiparti Gram Panchayat, the union enjoys a decisive majority as, besides ward members, it controls even the position of Sarpanch. As far as the location of the selected Gram Panchayats is concerned, Gummagatta Gram Panchayat is located in Gummagatta Mandal of Rayadurgam taluk of Anantapur district where the intervention of YIP is four years old. The remaining two Gram Panchayats are situated in Somandepalli Mandal of Anantapur district where the intervention of the YIP is nearly eight years old.

GUMMAGATTA GRAM PANCHAYAT

Gummagatta Gram Panchayat has only one village under its area of jurisdiction. The total number of households is 306. Across

TABLE 6.1 : NUMBER OF UNION MEMBERS ELECTED AS GRAM PANCHAYAT WARD MEMBERS AND SARPANCHES ACROSS THE PROJECT DISTRICTS

Sl. No.	*District*	*No. of Mandals*	*Ward seats won*		*Sarpanch seats won*		*Disabled candidates who won*		
			Total	*Women*	*Total*	*Women*	*Sarpanch*	*Ward*	*Total*
1.	Anantapur	46	2,237	700	178	50	3	5	8
2.	Chittoor/Nellore	33	1,815	602	200	70	-	20	20
3.	Nalgonda	20	987	286	82	34	3	-	3
4.	Cuddapah	8	241	66	19	8	-	-	-
5.	Kurnool	14	340	141	32	14	-	-	-
	TOTAL	121	5,620	1,795	511	176	6	25	31

Source: Records of YIP.

the different caste groups, Kurubas are in higher proportion than the others. The Kuruba community of this village is dependent on dual occupations—cultivation and *kambli* (woollen blanket) weaving—for their livelihood. YIP has been working here for the past three years. The size of the union membership is 702.

Composition of the Gram Panchayat

The Gummagatta Gram Panchayat consists of 10 ward members and one Sarpanch. Out of 10 members, five belong to the YIP union. Out of ten, three are women. Six, out of ten members, are from backward caste groups. The remaining (two each) are from forward and scheduled caste groups.

Profile of Members and Sarpanch

Out of the five Ward members belonging to the union, data were collected from four members and the Sarpanch during the field visits. The Ward members are Chinamallappa, Tilisurappa, Marekka and Basamma, and the Sarpanch is Konerappa.

(a) Chinamallappa belongs to Kuruba community and has studied up to SSLC. He owns four acres of wet land and two acres of dry land and also runs a fair price shop in the village. In addition, he is engaged in the traditional occupation, namely, *kambli* weaving. Chinamallappa is a member of the Congress party for the past 20 years and is also the secretary of the Fair Price Shop Dealers Association at the Mandal level. He got elected to the Gram Panchayat unanimously by promising street lights, installation of hand-pumps, repair of taps, latrines for women and house *pattas*. Before the completion of the five-year term, Chinamallappa also intends to use the position of Ward Membership for getting a job to his graduate son. While Chinamallappa has had no previous experience in the Panchayat, his mother was a nominated member for two terms. He has been associated with the YIP union for the past three years.

(b) Tilisurappa also got elected to the Gram Panchayat unanimously by promising to initiate measures to solve the water problems and construct latrines for women. He has studied up to Intermediate and belongs to the washerman caste. He owns

0.70 acre of wet land and 0.60 acre of dry land. He has been associated with the YIP union for the past three years.

(c) Marekka is illiterate and has been elected to the Panchayat unanimously. She belongs to the Kuruba community. She is also the president of DWCRA group and is engaged in *kambli* weaving. Marekka was not interested in participating in the elections. Actually, it was her husband who was the real aspirant for the position. Since the ward membership was reserved for backward caste women, Marekka was persuaded to contest the post of Ward member. Throughout the interview with her, the responses came from Marekka's husband on her behalf. Marekka and her husband are associated with the YIP union for the past three years.

(d) Basamma is also illiterate and belongs to the scheduled caste community. She works as an agricultural wage labourer. She has no previous experience and got elected unanimously. Basamma's son works as a part-time electrician for Gummagatta Gram Panchayat. Basamma has been associated with the YIP union for the past three and half years.

(e) The Sarpanch of Gummagatta Gram Panchayat is Konerappa who belongs to the Kuruba community. At the time of election, Konerappa was not associated with the YIP union and subsequently, became a member. He is around 55 years old and got elected to the Gram Panchayat for the first time with a majority of 490 votes. He has studied up to 5th class. He owns 10 acres of land. However, since there are no irrigation facilities available, he has been able to cultivate only three to four acres. According to the Sarpanch, the pressing needs of the people of Gummagatta are roads, latrines for women, street lights and drinking water.

Participation and functioning of Members

The Gummagatta Gram Panchayat met four times after its constitution. The first meeting focused on oath taking ceremony of the Sarpanch and Ward members. The second meeting of Gram Panchayat was convened to discuss about works to be undertaken under the Jawahar Rozgar Yojana (JRY), when a grant of Rs. 9,000 was sanctioned. According to the Ward members from the union, the circular about the meeting was sent a day prior to its conduct. The circular, the members informed, did not comprise of the agenda or reasons for convening the meeting. It was only at the venue of the meeting that the agenda was informed to the members. Though the purpose of the meeting was to discuss the works to be undertaken, it, in reality, ended by merely ratifying the proposal of the Sarpanch for the construction of a latrine and bathroom for the Gram Panchayat. The Ward members from the union neither sought time nor objected to pass the resolution. The issue was also not discussed with the Mandal secretary in the union meeting.

The Vice-Sarpanch was elected during the course of the third meeting. He was elected amid confusion, infighting and was dominated by a few influential persons of the village. Though the Vice-Sarpanch's post is not reserved for scheduled caste women, Basamma got elected to the post without even being a contender for the post!

Despite the policy of the YIP to capture the Vice-Sarpanch post wherever there is a non-union Sarpanch, Basamma got elected by accident to the post rather than through a very well thought out strategy. All the three male Ward members from the union and Marekka's husband competed with each other and could not arrive at a consensus. Basamma was not a contender for the post; but her name was suggested by Peda Reddy (one of the wealthy and influential persons of Gummagatta) and was seconded by former Karnam (Village Accountant). It may be quite relevant to note here that both Peda Reddy and Karnam are not members of the Gram Panchayat but attend the meetings whenever crucial decisions are to be taken. The Sarpanch does not appear to be very assertive and, according to the Ward members, often succumbs to the pressure of influential persons. The Ward members from the union have neither protested nor objected against the role of outsiders in Panchayat meetings.

The fourth meeting was organised to pass a resolution seeking purchase of some furniture—chairs—for the Gram Panchayat and to undertake minor repairs. On the other hand, the pro-poll promises made by the union Ward members and also the Sarpanch were quite different. Although they promised street lights and solving the water crisis, a decision was taken for spending the money on furnitures.

All the male members of the Gram Panchayat attended all the four meetings conducted. Among the three women members, Basamma attended all the meetings, Marekka attended the first meeting and was represented by her husband for the second and third meetings. The intimation about the fourth meeting was not sent to her except the register seeking the signature to ratify the resolution passed for purchasing furnitures. The other woman member belonging to the forward caste has not attended any of the meetings conducted and was represented by her husband, but the register was sent to the house for collecting the signature.

Though the Sarpanch of the Gram Panchayat enjoys the *de jure* authority to convene the meetings, all the four meetings held were called and conducted by the Village Development Officer (VDO). It was the VDO who sent the intimation about the meetings to Sarpanch two days in advance without any details about the agenda. Actually, according to the provisions of the Panchayat Raj Act, the bureaucracy—whether VDO or Mandal Development Officer (MDO)—can intervene and conduct a meeting only when the Sarpanch fails to organise ordinary meetings at least once in three months. Further, even after one year of constitution, the seal and records of Gram Panchayat were not handed over to the Sarpanch. This is the case with almost all the Gram Panchayats located in Gummagatta Mandal. Though the seal and records are not handed over, the Mandal level union executive committee has neither taken up the issue nor the Gram Panchayat members passed any resolution seeking the same.

PANDIPARTI GRAM PANCHAYAT

The Pandiparti Gram Panchayat has two villages under its geographical area of operation: Manchepalli and Pandiparti. Manchepalli village has 150 households and 600 voters. The village is heterogeneous in terms of social composition. Most of the households in this village belong to the Muslim community, backward caste groups like Boya, Kuruba and Bestha and scheduled castes. In numerical terms, the proportion of households belonging to scheduled castes is slightly higher than those belonging to the other groups.

There are 300 households and nearly 1,300 voters in Pandiparti village. Out of 300 households, about 100 belong to the scheduled castes and the remaining belong to backward and forward castes. Almost all the households in both the villages are sub-marginal, marginal, small and medium farmers and depend upon both cultivation and agricultural wage labour for livelihood. During the lean season, the scheduled caste households of Manchepalli work as railway coolies.

Composition of the Gram Panchayat

The Pandiparti Gram Panchayat has ten Ward members and one Sarpanch. Out of ten members, four belong to scheduled castes and three to backward and forward castes. Four, out of ten members, are women. Five Ward members and Sarpanch are associated with the YIP union for the past four to six years. The Sarpanch's post in the recently held election was reserved for scheduled caste women. Until recently, the position of the Sarpanch was controlled by members of Reddy caste. For the first time, due to reservation, the position has come to be controlled by other caste group and that too by a woman.

Profile of Members and Sarpanch

For the purpose of this study, the Sarpanch Thimmakka, Vice-Sarpanch, two female members Anjanamma and Ashwatamma and two male members—Rangaiah and Mylaram, were interviewed.

(a) The Sarpanch Thimmakka, aged around 33 years, has no previous political experience and got elected to the Panchayat for the first time. Thimmakka belongs to the scheduled caste group and was elected unanimously. Her family owns three acres of dry land. Apart from cultivating own land, Thimmakka works as both agricultural and non-agricultural labourer. Thimmakka hails from Manchepalli village and has been associated with the YIP union for the past four years.

(b) The Vice-Sarpanch, aged around 22 years, belongs to the Reddy caste group. He has studied up to 10th class, and does not belong to the YIP Union. He lives in Bangalore and is currently working in Khoday's sugar factory. He visits the village on the 14th day of every month to attend the Panchayat meeting. The Vice-Sarpanch's father is a fair price shop owner and in fact the original aspirant for the post. He, however, did not contest out of fear of losing the fair price shop dealership.

(c) Ashwatamma, aged around 32, got elected to the Panchayat for the first time due to reservation. Ashwatamma, an illiterate and a housewife, is a member of the YIP union of Manchepalli for the past two years. Gurrappa, the husband of Ashwatamma, responded to all our queries on her behalf.

(d) Anjanamma, aged 30, also got elected to the Panchayat for the first time. She is illiterate and depends solely on agricultural wage labour for her livelihood.

(e) Mylaram, aged between 32-35 years, also got elected to the Panchayat for the first time. He is not educated. Mylaram depends on both cultivation and agricultural wage labour for livelihood. He has been associated with the YIP union of Manchepalli for the past five years.

(f) Rangaiah, aged between 40-45, got elected to the Panchayat as Ward member due to reservation for backward castes. He belongs to Bajantri (Barber) caste and has studied up to 5th class. Rangaiah owns 4 acres of dry land and 1/2 acre of wet land. In addition to cultivation, he is also engaged in the traditional occupation of barber community. Rangaiah, though not associated with the YIP union, agrees with the model. He, however, expressed dissatisfaction about the mode of functioning of unions in Pandiparti and Manchepalli.

Participation and functioning of Members

The Gram Panchayat has met four times—as per the information provided by the Manchepalli union members—during the period August 1995 to December 1996. The meetings were held alternatively at Manchepalli and Pandiparti as the Panchayat area covers these two villages. Though the Gram Panchayat has its own building, the meetings are conducted normally in the school or community hall as the former Sarpanch is using it as his storage place and has not handed over the keys to the newly elected Sarpanch. He has also not handed over the seal and records of the Gram Panchayat. However, none of the ward members from the YIP union has raised this issue either in the monthly meeting of the village or mandal level executive committee.

The first Panchayat meeting was conducted to take the oath and elect a Vice-Sarpanch. Though the union is in a strong position with five Ward members and Sarpanch, a non-union member was elected as Vice-Sarpanch. This was much against the YIP's advocacy that wherever the union is in a strong position, efforts should be made to capture the post of Vice-Sarpanch as well. This, however, is not a difficult task as the election of Vice-Sarpanch is indirect and Ward members elect/select the person.

What transpired in Pandiparti, however, was different. Ever since the Gram Panchayat came into existence in the village, the position of the Sarpanch was retained by upper caste, rich and large landowners of Pandiparti village. With the policy of reservations, a scheduled caste woman got elected. As a way of maintaining the power balance, a Reddy non-union Ward member from Pandiparti was elected to the Vice-Sarpanch's post. It is quite interesting to note here that the nomination was made by the union member Mr. Gurrappa—husband and representative of the Ward member Ashwatamma.

The second and third meetings apparently have passed the resolution to install street lights in Harijan street of Manchepalli village, and to widen the road between Manchepalli and the neighbouring village of Brahmanapalli. The fourth meeting has come out with a long list of resolutions. However, before listing out the resolutions passed in the meeting, it is interesting to examine the issues like how the meeting was organised, who conducted the meeting and decided the agenda, sitting positions of various members, the level of participation in the discussions by various members and the role played by them at the meeting. Such an exercise is considered essential as it would help one in understanding the role and participation levels of different members.

The meeting was scheduled to begin at 9 a.m. in the community hall of Pandiparti village. The venue, however, was shifted to the school as the foodgrain bags of fair price shop had to be unloaded into the community hall. In order to facilitate the meeting, the school teachers suspended the classes for three hours.

The members who participated in the meeting were Sarpanch—Thimmakka, and ward members Anjanamma, Rangaiah, Mylaram, Ramaiah and Vice-Sarpanch. Ashwatamma and one upper caste woman member (Pandiparti) were represented by their respective husbands—Gurrappa and Ramakrishna Reddy. The Sarpanch sat in a corner and remained a passive observer. The Manchepalli village union president, Mr. Nagabushanam, played the role of Sarpanch during the meeting. The Vice-Sarpanch was moving in and out of the meeting hall and his father acted as his spokesperson. Interestingly, as soon as we reached the village, the father of the Vice-Sarpanch approached us and introduced himself as the Vice-Sarpanch. It was only later that his actual position became known. Reacting to the comment of a member about the aloofness of the Sarpanch, the union president, Mr. Nagabushanam declared that, "I am the real Sarpanch and I shall conduct the meeting". In addition, the former Karnam, Swamy, who has been drafting the minutes of the Panchayat meetings for the past five years was also there. Swamy, however, was very clear about his role and essentially confined himself to the job of drafting and restrained from offering opinion or comments on any issue. For instance, to a request regarding the tax to be levied on shops and business establishments, Swamy refused by noting that it is the members who should take the decisions and not the outsiders like him.

The Sarpanch is a very diffident person and not aware of any procedure concerning the meetings. Being an experienced person, Swamy not only prepared the agenda but also advised her not to sign on any white paper. The agenda, as prepared by Swamy, had four points: approval of income and expenditure statement, repair of Panchayat office, collection of house tax and others. The members and union president added some more issues to the agenda. They are furnitures for Panchayat office, rise in the sweeper's salary, completion of a drainage canal in Manchepalli, and power of countersigning the cheques.

The agenda was discussed essentially by the union president, the father of Vice-Sarpanch, Rangaiah, Gurrappa (husband of Ashwatamma) and Ramakrishna Reddy (husband of an upper caste woman). In the course of the meeting, union president, Gurrappa held a mini discussion outside the meeting hall separately for about half-an-hour. The attempts of Mylaram and the other member to intervene proved in vain due to the overbearing behaviour of the union president and Gurrappa. Gurrappa and the union president were so active that they nominated and seconded the name of the Vice-Sarpanch for putting the counter-signature on cheques along with the Sarpanch. The union president even submitted some bills purported to be related to the Panchayat expenditure for the month of January. The Sarpanch remained a passive observer throughout the meeting and it was towards the end that she pleaded with Swamy to include a resolution concerning the laying of slabs near a well in Manchepalli. According to the villagers and union members, the union president and Gurrappa are attempting to dominate the meetings as they were the original aspirants for the position of Sarpanch and the ward member respectively. They, however, could not contest due to the reservation of both the positions for scheduled and backward caste women.

Resolutions passed

1. Approval of income and expenditure statement for the month of January.
2. Purchase of twelve chairs, two tables and carpets for Gram Panchayat office.
3. Revision of house tax.
4. Preparation of the list of newly constructed houses for the purpose of levying taxes.

5. Levy of annual tax of Rs. 20 on shops and business establishments which obtained licence from the Panchayat office.
6. Repair of the Panchayat office.
7. Conferring the power of counter-signing of the cheque to the Vice-Sarpanch.

While no discussion took place on income and expenditure statement, the furnitures, house tax and tax on shops were discussed at length by the members. The discussion on counter-signing cheque power was held outside the meeting hall and neither the Sarpanch nor the members participated in it. Further, though three meetings (prior to 14/02/1996) were claimed to have been held, in reality, only one (oath taking ceremony) was conducted. According to the villagers, the union president and a few members wrote down the minutes and obtained the signatures without the meetings actually conducted.

NAGINAYINI CHERUVU GRAM PANCHAYAT

The Naginayini Cheruvu Gram Panchayat has three villages in its area of operation. They are Naginayini Cheruvu, Naginayini Cheruvu Thanda and Busayagaripalli. The Naginayini Cheruvu village has 100 households. The village consists of backward caste group mainly Besthas. Most of the households have marginal and small holdings and depend on both cultivation and agricultural wage labour.

The Naginayini Cheruvu Thanda has about 100 households and consists of only the scheduled tribe group—Nayak. The households of Naginayini Cheruvu Thanda appeared to be quite well off and have *pucca* buildings. The appearance of some of the houses is so good that they have overhead tanks and telephone connections and can be compared with those in a city's posh locality. Most of the households of the Thanda own land and the range varies from 10 to 400 acres. Interestingly, the tribal group of Nayaks of Thanda—who owned around 40 to 50 acres of land about 15 to 20 years back—now own nearly 300 to 400 acres of cultivable land around the village. Being the owners of small and marginal holdings, the people of Naginayini Cheruvu are dependent on medium and large farmers of Thanda for credit and wage employment. It was the dependency on credit which appeared to have resulted in land transfers—an outcome of mortgage and adjustment against the loans borrowed.

Busayagaripalli village has 90 households and 300 voters. Out of 90, nearly 60 households, with the exception of two, have either marginal or small holdings and belong to the backward caste—Bestha. Only two households do not own land and solely depend on wage employment. The remaining 30 households own medium and large holdings and belong to the Reddy caste.

Composition of the Gram Panchayat

The Gram Panchayat consists of eight Ward members and one Sarpanch. Out of eight members, three hail from Naginayini Cheruvu Thanda; two from Busayagaripalli; and three from Naginayini Cheruvu. Out of eight, five members are women and five have association with the YIP union.

Profile of Members and Sarpanch

Information was collected from Sarpanch—Narayanapa, Ward members—Laxmi Bai, Rami Bai, Venkataramamma, Anjanappa, Kistappa and Bhanumantam.

(a) The Sarpanch, Narayanappa is not a union member. He won the election by defeating two union members. The post of the Sarpanch until the recent election was controlled by Pila Nayak from Thanda. As the post was reserved for backward caste men, Narayanappa contested with the support of the former Sarpanch of Thanda. Narayanappa has studied up to 7th class and owns 4 acres of land. He has no previous political experience.

(b) Laxmi Bai, a Ward member, belongs to Naginayini Cheruvu Thanda. Laxmi Bai got elected unopposed from a general seat. Laxmi Bai originally had no intention of participating in the election. She accompanied another woman Rami Bai to give moral support at the time of filing the nomination papers. It so happened that no one turned up to file the nomination for a general seat in Naginayini Cheruvu Gram Panchayat. The election officer suggested to her to file the nomination.

Laxmi Bai belongs to the age group of 55-60 and has studied up to 5th class. She has four sons. Two sons are employed in public and private sector companies, one is a cultivator and the other is studying B.Sc. Laxmi Bai's family owns 15 acres of land. She works on her lands along with the other family members. Laxmi Bai is related to the Sarpanch of erstwhile Gram Panchayat.

Laxmi Bai is not a union member as she belongs to the rich farming community. However, she has been participating actively in various activities of unions including the *dharna* organised during February 1996, in front of the office of the Mandal revenue officer. She had been enrolled as a member of the union on the day we met her, by the group leader of the YIP.

Laxmi Bai appeared to be very articulate and clear about the village level politics. She informed, in the course of discussion, that the Sarpanch, Narayanappa, got elected because of the support extended by former Sarpanch and 300 voters of Naginayini Cheruvu Thanda. Now, after the election, the Sarpanch does not care for the Thanda members and conducts the meetings in the night time or informs the members just few hours before the meeting.

According to Laxmi Bai, the pressing problems of Naginayini Cheruvu Gram Panchayat are maintenance of roads, drainage canals and bore wells. Though Laxmi Bai appeared to be articulate and analytical, she, however, has no idea or plan of action about the problems of women and how a Panchayat with women members having majority can address them. In spite of prodding her about the issue, Laxmi Bai, however, could not think of any plan about tackling women's problems through the Panchayat. Further, Laxmi Bai seems to be having a bias towards wage discrimination followed between female and male wage labourers. The justification offered is that the work undertaken by women workers is lighter and work hours are shorter compared to the men workers.

(c) Rami Bai also hails from Naginayini Cheruvu Thanda and got elected unanimously to a reserved seat. Her family owns about three acres of land. She is engaged in both cultivation and agricultural wage labour. Rami Bai has been associated with the YIP union for the past three years. She also could not reflect much about the women oriented programmes that can be undertaken within the purview of Gram Panchayat activities.

(d) Venkataramamma hails from Busayagaripalli village. She is not educated and can only sign her name. Venkataramamma works as an agricultural wage labourer. She has been associated with the union for the past three years. Venkataramamma's husband was a member of the erstwhile Gram Panchayat. As the seat has been reserved for a backward caste woman, Venkataramamma participated in the election.

(e) Anjanappa, hailing from Busayagaripalli, has studied up to 10th class. Anjanappa's family owns about 7 acres of land and a *pucca* house. Some of his brothers are employed with the Government of Andhra Pradesh. Anjanappa has been a member of the union ever since it was established. Anjanappa is the president of the village union. Prior to becoming the president, he was a staff member of the YIP. According to Anjanappa, the pressing need of the villagers of Busayagaripalli is laying of road as it is causing considerable hardship to the mobility of the people.

(f) Kistappa hails from Naginayini Cheruvu main village and got elected to a backward caste seat reserved for men. He is not educated and belongs to the toddy tapper community. Kistappa owns five acres of land and grows groundnut and gingelly seeds. He also sells toddy and earns around Rs. 32 per day as wages. Kistappa has been a member of the union for the past four years.

(g) Bhanumantam, aged around 35, also belongs to Naginayini Cheruvu village. He has studied up to eighth class and has been a member of the union for the past six years. Bhanumantam got elected unanimously. He belongs to the Bestha community and owns three acres of land.

Participation and functioning of Members

Between August and December 1996, the Gram Panchayat met four times. The first meeting was concerned with oath taking ceremony of the Sarpanch and Ward members. The Vice-Sarpanch was elected during the second meeting. Though the YIP union controls five out of eight Ward seats, the position of the Vice-Sarpanch has gone to a non-union woman member from Naginayini Cheruvu Thanda. According to Anjanappa, there was no time to discuss the issue with other union members of the Panchayat as the meeting was convened hurriedly. Further, four ward members, especially women (both union and non-union), could not participate as the meeting was held in the night around 9 p.m. Interestingly, nobody, even the Ward members from the union objected to the timing of the meeting or absence of four members.

The third meeting discussed the carry-over balance of JRY funds of Rs. 3,500 and passed the resolution to take up the lane paving and repair of drainage canal in Naginayini Cheruvu village. The fourth meeting was convened to discuss the issues to be raised in the Mandal level Sarpanch's meeting, organised by the Mandal Development Officer.

CONCLUSIONS

The points that emerge from the foregoing discussion of the primary data on profile, participation and functioning are two fold. Firstly, the membership and executive positions of Gram Panchayats have come to be occupied by women, backward and scheduled caste persons. In other words, reservation has empowered the marginalized sections hitherto deprived of political power positions. Secondly, mere occupation and control of political positions by marginalised sections, however, has not resulted in their active and effective participation and exercising of decision making powers. This is, in spite of the association and exposure of members and office bearers of Panchayats with unions and unionisation process.

Speaking in general terms, the ability of the marginalised sections to exercise newly conferred power depends on the nature of their interaction with the forces operating in the larger village environmental set-up. But, given the number of years of intervention of the NGO and the association of Panchayat, Ward and executive members with the unions and unionisation, the role of village elite and bureaucracy should have been minimal. The very fact that the village elite could exercise large extent of influence over Panchayat affairs also indicates problems and complexities involved in organising the unorganised with a diverse social base.

Firstly, the Gram Panchayats in the state of Andhra Pradesh were constituted six months after the elections were over due to a stay order from the High Court on the issue of reservation. Secondly, Panchayats throughout the state of Andhra Pradesh are languishing for want of funds. Development activities in the state have come to a standstill as the ruling TDP government has been diverting the funds to fulfil the election promises of supplying highly subsidised rice and prohibition. Subsequently, prohibition has been removed, the price of subsidised rice has gone up. Further, whatever little funds available are spent by the government directly under the schemes like 'Shramadan' and 'Prajala Vaddaku Palana,' marginalising the Gram Panchayats in the process. As the funds made available to the Panchayats are only small, and were obtained from the Central Government's programme of JRY, the Panchayats in the state, leave alone the sample ones, could meet only a few times. In fact, this is one of the constraints faced in this study as attending several Gram Panchayat meetings became difficult.

In the case of sample Gram Panchayats, the superseding role played by bureaucracy and the former bastions of power positions, i.e., the rich landlords, and the aspirants of power from among the marginalised sections and YIP unions, have also affected the functioning of Gram Panchayats. These factors may be affecting the functioning of the Gram Panchayats in other parts of YIP's project districts and the state. Though the issues like the role of bureaucracy and rich landlords have not been taken up, the YIP has initiated certain measures to counter the negative impact of government programmes on the functioning of Gram Panchayats. It has initiated campaigns against the Government schemes like 'Shramadan' and 'Prajala Vaddaku Palana' and opposed prohibition. It filed a writ petition in the Supreme Court seeking the quashing of 'Prajala Vaddaku Palana'. In order to enable the newly elected Gram Panchayat members to participate effectively, the YIP has also conducted one to three days training camps for Sarpanches and Ward members separately to equip them with information on statutory provisions with assistance from the CAPART. Realising the limitations of one-time training, the YIP is also planning to undertake periodic follow-up and monitoring of the functioning of those Gram Panchayats which are numerically dominated by the unions. The monitoring and follow-up training are to be undertaken by the Mandal coordinators/secretaries with the advisory assistance of group leaders and district coordinators/ secretaries. As both the measures are still in planning stage, one has to wait for some more time to examine how empowered the marginalised sections have become.

NOTE

1. The study was conducted in seven Gram Panchayats selected from one of the oldest and from one of the newest Mandals of one of the oldest project districts (Anantapur) during the period August 1995 to March 1997. Gram Panchayats from each of the Mandals were selected by considering the numerical strength of the union members at the Ward and executive levels and in consultation with the YIP staff at the mandal level. The Panchayats thus selected were classified into four categories: (1) Panchayats where a majority of the Ward positions are held by uuion members and Sarpanch is captured by non-union Sarpanch; (2) Panchayats where Sarpanch's position as well as a majority of the Ward positions are held by union members; (3) Panchayats where union members consist of minorities; and (4) Panchayats without any representation from the unions promoted by the YIP.

7

PRAXIS's EXPERIENCE IN GRAM PANCHAYAT ELECTIONS

ALEX TUSCANO

BACKGROUND OF THE TARGET AREA

Praxis is working in Devanahalli Taluk and in parts of Bangalore North and Doddaballapur Taluks in Bangalore Rural District in Karnataka where Dalits are in large numbers. In spite of the fact that this target area is very close to the metropolitan city of Bangalore, significant backwardness among the poor is observed. There have been innumerable cases of oppression of the Dalits by Vokkaligas, who are the dominant landowners. A majority of the Dalits own between half-an-acre to one acre of dry land and they have to depend on wage labour for their livelihood.

The literacy level among thc women is very low, 90 per cent of the women in the age group of above 25 are illiterate. Similarly, more than 70 per cent of the men in the age group of above 30 are illiterate. The cases of child bonded labour are rather high in the area. This is primarily due to the indebtedness of Dalits to the landlords. Coupled with this the conditions of women are at sub-human level. They are not only exploited and oppressed by the upper castes, but are also victims of atrocities by their drunkard husbands.

PRAXIS's INVOLVEMENT WITH THE PEOPLE

Praxis has been working with these people for the last ten years. The main objective of Praxis's involvement has been:

1. building a mass organisation of the poor by educating the poor and forming Sanghas among them at the village level;
2. to empower the poor and bring them into the mainstream

of political life by making them actively participate in Panchayat Raj elections and building themselves as a united vote bank (constituency) which will empower them to offer support to a political candidate or a party that will work for their interest;

3. to ensure the development of women by organising them and making them to work for equal opportunities with men and for justice;
4. building institutional and economic resource base among the poor through training and encouraging the people to undertake income generating programmes; and
5. to promote environmental regeneration and sustainable agriculture.

To achieve these objectives, PRAXIS has undertaken the following programmes:

1. Educating people, i.e., men and women, by conducting regular weekly Sangha meetings at the village level.
2. Organising training programmes to promote leadership and developing management capabilities among the Sangha members.
3. Conducting savings and credit programmes and income generating programmes. Special emphasis is given for income generation programmes for the poorest women.
4. Providing supplementary education for school-going children and encouraging girl child education.
5. Improving the quality of the land of the poor by undertaking programmes for land levelling, conservation of soil and water.

Apart from this, PRAXIS has been working to ensure implementation of 'Employment Assurance Scheme through lobbying and advocacy by becoming part of district and state NGO networks.

PRAXIS's ROLE IN PANCHAYAT RAJ ELECTIONS

Active participation in the Gram Panchayat election was PRAXIS's first experience. Earlier to this, sympathy was shown for one or the other candidate in the assembly elections. As far as elections were concerned, NGOs were not allowed to involve in party politics and elections, PRAXIS had kept the interest in election only at this level.

According to PRAXIS's conviction, development has to be understood in political terms. It is only the political power that determines the shape of the destiny of the people. When political power is vested in the hands of the wealthy class, it will only defend their own economic interests.

To bring about development from the point of view of the poor, they need to be in the mainstream of politics. They should be in a position to choose the government that will develop an economic system which will bring about social justice. This calls for political empowerment of the poor.

In the present situation, whoever had been elected from the Dalit and the poor class there is a tendency to join the ruling class or become puppets in the hands of the ruling class. Hence, the question of electing leaders from the exploited class does not automatically solve the problems of the poor and exploited.

The skills needed to participate in the government among the poor and the Dalits are not yet developed to the required extent. Wherever there are skilled politicians from Dalit and poor class in the government, they are no different from the politicians from the ruling class.

In the light of the above, when one talks about elections to Gram Panchayats and the poor, one has to recognise that there are several tasks ahead. There is a need to give political education to the exploited class and to understand the new kind of politics which departs from the hitherto existing political culture and values. Political authority and power should aim at removing disparities in the society. The power is not meant for the purpose of gaining more power and continue in power. Nor should the political power be meant to enhance the economic system that has failed to bring any benefits to the majority of the poor.

At present, the option we have is to elect the government that will be responsible to the people. If it fails to respond to people's demands, then it should be brought down. In order to do this, poor should be united and conscious of their long term interests.

The poor and the Dalits hold considerable votes that can be decisive for getting anyone elected. The decisive nature of the united voting could make the prospective candidate to agree upon to fulfil the demands of the poor. The 'election manifesto' should be drafted by the electorate and elect the rulers who agree to implement the manifesto.

In this context, PRAXIS's slogan would be 'unite and vote unitedly' and the organisation intends to move in this direction of political involvement. It is a long journey.

At another level, it is thought that the organisation could work at the Gram Panchayat level both to elect the desirable members and also get elected to the Panchayats.

At the present level of development, the Dalits and the poor from the villages are not able to participate and get elected to the state assemblies. The Panchayats are the only government bodies that are within their reach. These elections are seen both as opportunity to capture power at the lower level and also to learn about politics and acquire skills to become politicians for the future—politicians with a difference!

The Gram Panchayat election is an ideal situation where the candidates do not fight along the party lines. Many dedicated persons not linked to the existing political parties could contest in the elections. It offers the challenge to the leaders from the exploited class to get involved in the local government bodies and ensure that the opportunities available at the local government for the development of the poor are utilised to the maximum.

PRAXIS's EXPERIENCE WITH GRAM PANCHAYAT ELECTIONS

Before the Gram Panchayat elections, PRAXIS made a year long campaign in 150 villages of Devanahalli taluk. The campaign was at different levels. On the one hand, PRAXIS had to give the Sangha members information about the Panchayat elections, and also had to explain to them the new Panchayat Raj bill that had been enacted.

PRAXIS also participated in the workshop conducted by Vistar and Federation of Voluntary Organisations in Rural Development in Karnataka (FEVORD-K) on the Panchayat Raj Act. This helped the selected members to get a fairly good knowledge of the Act. PRAXIS was able to get documentation to be used for the education of the activists and the Sangha members. There were two rounds of training for all the activists. This made the activists competent enough to conduct meetings and give this information to the villagers.

At the second level, PRAXIS organised training programmes for the Sangha leaders and representatives. There was a special training programme organised for women. At the third level, PRAXIS had village level meetings to explain to the Sangha members about the Panchayat Raj Act. At the fourth level, PRAXIS had to convince the Sangha members that they have now the opportunity to capture power at the Gram Panchayat level.

To bring this point home to them the first point that was argued was that so far poor in the project area voted for either the Congress or the Janata Dal, which have not brought about any change in their lives. This is the time to vote for themselves. Instead of voting for any party, they need to vote for their own organisation, i.e., Sangha.

Dalits constitute 30 per cent of the population in the taluk and along with them there are scores of other poor. All of them should get together and vote for the representatives from within their own class. This ensures that at least 30 per cent of the Gram Panchayat members would comprise of the enlightened leaders from the downtrodden class. Apart from this, the poor also have the opportunity to elect those candidates from the upper class whom they find desirable.

While campaigning and educating the poor, PRAXIS used street plays, songs and other local popular media. Through these cultural programmes, PRAXIS explained how the politicians are misusing the people's votes and not doing anything after winning the election; how the poor people cast their votes just for a packet of arrack or a sari; how the politicians break the unity of the poor in a village; and how the politicians exploit the poor by not implementing the anti-poverty schemes which are meant for them. PRAXIS's main aim was to make people aware of the value of their votes and how it can really help them in electing the right candidate who can do good for them; to expose all those vested elements in the society who exploited the poor after getting their votes. These campaigns and awareness programmes helped to make the people think about nominating candidates who can do good for them.

As a consequence of the above mentioned programmes, the Dalits decided not to receive liquor and other forms of corrupt incentives from the upper class. A detailed discussion took place among themselves to work towards having a representative in the Gram Panchayat who can speak and do things for the poor.

Meanwhile, PRAXIS field staff went to the Taluk office and collected information about the Gram Panchayat elections, seat distribution and reserved seats. This was discussed in every Sangha meeting and the people were asked to choose their candidates to contest in the election. The people chose their candidates and the nomination papers were filed in the Gram Panchayat headquarters.

The selection of candidates was not a smooth process. Many wanted to stand for the election. In the whole process, there were some difficulties also. In selecting the candidates in Bijjwara, Savakanahalli, Karahalli and Battramarenahalli, the Sangha people could not come to any consensus.

— In Bijjawara, Sanghas's Taluk Level President, Krishnappa, joined hands with the village upper caste rich people and worked against the official candidate chosen by the Sangha members in the elections.
— In Karahalli, Shanthamma was selected as the candidate but the upper caste members succeeded in manipulating Chowdamma, another member of the Sangha, to contest against her own Sangha member, Shanthamma.
— In Savakanahalli also, the upper castes succeeded in dividing the poor (Box 7.1).
— In Battramarenahalli, Lakshmamma, a Sangha member, was opposed by another Sangha member who was foisted by the upper castes which resulted in the defeat of the NGO candidate.

As stated earlier, this was PRAXIS's first experience in participating in the selection process. There were many things which were not clear to the organisers.

BOX 7.1: SAVAKANAHALLI

Savakanahalli village is situated about 5 Kms. away from Devanahalli town. The population of this village is composed of Vokkaligas, Bovis, Naiks and Harijans. Though there are 120 Dalit families, they constitute one-third of the total population.

PRAXIS has been working primarily with the Harijans who have organised themselves into a relatively strong Sangha. With the collaboration of PRAXIS they have also built a Sangha house. The Savings and Credit programme has been functioning well. There were three contenders for the Panchayat membership from among the Sangha members—Muniyellamma, Muniyamma and Rathnamma. All the three were equally committed and capable persons. The Sangha unanimously selected Muniyellamma to be the candidate. All the Sangha members were confident that Muniyellamma would win the election. They also got the support of the STs who were not Sangha members.

But on the day of filing the nomination, Sollapuri Muniyamma, another Dalit woman, was taken to the Returning Officer by the landlord Patel of this village and made to file the nomination. This was something which the Sangha members never expected. Sollapuri Muniyamma was a member of the Sangha and her husband who is a chronic asthmatic patient has received lot of help from the Sangha. However, she had gone over to the side of the landlords. Ten more Dalit families also came forward in support of Sollapuri Muniyamma. In the election, though all the Sangha members, having about 400 votes, voted for Muniyellamma, the entire Vokkaliga community voted for Sollapuri Muniyamma.

Given the nature of election procedures, when Dalits are in a majority and even if they have a strong Sangha, they may not win the election when there is even a single member who goes against the Sangha.

1. The Ward system is very different from the system of constituency. As a result, PRAXIS was misled. While the Sangha members held more than sufficient number of votes required for winning the election, the election was lost because of the Ward system.
2. The upper caste, upper class members had the opportunity to defeat the NGO candidate. To give an example, in Savakanahalli, the official candidate got the required number of votes as per the Sangha calculation. But the candidate from the Dalit foisted by the upper castes and fielded against the official candidate could win the election on the votes of the upper castes. This could happen only because of the Ward system where the votes of the upper castes could tilt the balance.
3. The realisation of the Ward system came too late. The second realisation that came to the organisation was that though the election was not held along the party symbols, people behaved and voted on the basis of the party affiliation of the candidates. The party consciousness was not high among the Sangha members except for two or three villages.

Last minute alliances were made with people from the upper castes to ensure that because of their voting pattern the Sangha candidates did not lose. This worked in three villages.

Totally, Sangha members contested 42 seats and were successful in 22 of them. Interestingly, in Kaggalahalli, a woman candidate managed to get elected unopposed (Box 7.2). This was for the general seat. After the elections, PRAXIS organised several training programmes to the Panchayat members. All the members belonging to different castes and communities were encouraged to participate in the training. Through this training programme, PRAXIS succeeded in winning over many more Panchayat members. It was important to increase the strength of the Dalits in the Panchayat. This effort gave very good results. This motivated many to become members of the Sanghas and almost all of them are making use of the Panchayat institution for the development of the Dalits by getting house sites, drinking water and sanitation facilities.

BOX 7.2: KAGGALAHALLI

Kaggalahalli, another village in Devanahalli Taluk, is situated about 30 Kms. from Bangalore. The village population is dominated by the Vokkaligas, about 3/4th of the total population.

The 75 Dalit families have a fairly well-knit Sangha. In this village, there was no reserved seat for the Dalits. Instead, there was one reserved seat for women under general category. The Sangha members decided to field Gowramma. An important characteristic was that no Dalit wanted to oppose the candidature of Gowramma. The Sangha members approached the Vokkaligas for their support for Gowramma. With a lot of bargaining the Vokkaligas agreed to let Gowramma win the election unopposed.

The significance of this case is that though the Vokkaligas have a conflicting relationship with the Dalits on other occasions, they had no problem in supporting Gowramma as both Dalit and Vokkaligas shared loyalties towards Congress Party. In general, though the party symbols were not involved in this Panchayat Raj elections, the party loyalties did play a role.

FUTURE PERSPECTIVES

Panchayat Raj and political empowerment of the poor

(a) Political empowerment of the exploited poor is the only fundamental path to development and change. PRIs are the most effective instruments in the process of empowerment of the poor. Given this potential, PRAXIS plans to:

(i) ensure effective functioning of the Gram Sabhas. The Gram Sabhas will give an opportunity for all to voice their demands. It makes them understand the way PRIs function. The Gram Sabha, in fact functions as a parliament, at the lowest level of social and political life. It also serves as a means to educate the people about their mass power to service the local government bodies;

(ii) see that the organisation (Sanghas) of the poor will bring pressure on the functioning of the PRIs to ensure participation of the people in Panchayat politics, and take up and successfully implement the development programmes meant for increasing the quality of life of the poor;

(iii) influence the Panchayat members elected from the upper caste/class to look at the development of the poor as an important function of the PRIs; and,

(iv) ensure fruitful and meaningful participation of women at all levels of PRIs, i.e., in the Gram Sabhas as well as in the Panchayats as its members.

(b) PRAXIS endeavours to ensure the election of socially committed persons to the PRIs. These people might be from the upper caste or from the exploited classes. By this the poor people should experience that if they stand united they can be 'King Makers'.

(c) Moving a step further from this, the PRAXIS tries to ensure that the committed leaders from within the exploited classes can be elected to the PRIs not only under reserved quotas but also under general category. In other words, the PRAXIS wants to move towards a situation where the poor people would develop themselves to a position to capture maximum power in the local government bodies.

(d) It is also intended to ensure that the PRIs also become a learning experience for the people :

(i) They will learn the skills of a committed politician who can participate in the running of a government and ensure the development of the poor people. In this process, the leaders from the exploited classes can be trained to participate in the Taluk Panchayat, Zilla Panchayat and even in the State Assembly elections.

(ii) Ultimately, the PRAXIS aims to unite all the poor, exploited and Dalits into one political force which can become powerful enough to determine the election of a person that they like to have. This also makes them powerful to get their charter of demands implemented by the political leaders they support.

To achieve all this, the PRAXIS visualises a sustained process of political education. The Sanghas that the organisation has built in the villages will be so steered that they will be able to achieve this political objective.

8

DEVELOPMENT OF POWER

NARINDER BEDI

INTRODUCTION

To Young India Project (YIP), the question of which development strategy can eradicate poverty, whether in rural or urban areas, cannot be answered without also addressing the question who has the power.

If poverty is the result of the concentration of productive assets in the hands of the politically powerful sections of the society, one cannot then talk about removal of poverty without questioning the concentration of assets and political power in the hands of a minority.

Development is not just the implementation of government's anti-poverty programmes. Development is the process by which the poor are enabled to participate in the implementation of those programmes in order to not only ensure their proper implementation but also to oppose the programmes which are not benefiting them.

'Participation' and 'Oppose' are basically power related terms. If government programmes have failed in the past, it is because people who are to benefit from them are powerless to ensure that development funds are not diverted. Unless they develop this power, the process of development in India will continue to produce disheartening results.

Everybody is attempting to come to power except the poor and this negates all efforts of poverty eradication in our country. Political parties are on the side of the rich and in support of *status quo*, i.e., in support of bourgeois capitalism[1]. If the rich and powerful are busy monopolising power to further their own interest, who is there to help the poor to empower themselves?

Unfortunately, NGOs are literally petrified of the word power. They do not want to undertake power related issues because they are afraid that the state will deprive them of their funds or harass them locally. They have, therefore, stayed away from taking up issues and problems of the poor in which power struggles are imminent.

The tendency among a large number of NGOs is that they would rather sacrifice the poor than their own comforts and security. But, our ten years of experience in organising the rural poor in Andhra Pradesh has convinced us that unless we and the poor together start involving ourselves in power struggles from grassroots levels upwards nothing is going to change.

We would very much like more NGOs especially those who claim to be committed to justice, equity and to the achieving of a society in which human rights are respected, to openly side with the poor in their struggle for power. For, just as bourgeois class cannot come to power without their parties, the poor cannot rise to power without the necessary ideological inputs and organisational skills which, at the present, only we can provide.

The writing is on the wall; but, how many NGOs are willing to read it?

PANCHAYAT RAJ INSTITUTIONS: OPPORTUNITIES

In 1993, the Government introduced the 73rd Amendment in order to bring PRIs under the Constitution. Before that, the elections to the Panchayat Raj at Gram, Mandal and Zilla were held if and when the state government chose to hold them. But, after the 73rd Amendment came into effect, it became mandatory that all state governments must hold Panchayat Raj elections every five years exactly like the parliament and the assembly elections.

Under the Act, the post of a state level election commissioner was created and he/she was made responsible to hold free and fair elections as per the Act. In addition, the Act under the Eleventh Schedule transferred as many as 29 responsibilities to the PRIs.

If the Act did not transfer all powers to the PRIs such as: law and order, freedom to collect whatever taxes they chose to, it at least made poverty eradication programmes and community development programmes the sole responsibility of the PRIs. For the first time since independence, the role of the PRIs from Zilla Parishad down to Gram Panchayat was clearly defined as development in all its aspects. In addition, reservations were given to SC, ST, BC and women who constituted the majority of the poor.

In Andhra Pradesh, traditionally, the Sarpanch of any Gram Panchayat has been a big landowner, by and large, either a Reddy or a Kamma, and SC, ST only under reservation. And even where there were SC, ST Sarpanches they were dummy Sarpanches, nominated and controlled by big landowning Reddy or Kamma. Even at the grassroots level power had never been enjoyed by the poor and they were always too afraid to challenge the powerful landlords on whom they depended for work, loans, and protection from the state. This dependence has a long and deep history.

But the 73rd Amendment and the subsequent passage of the Andhra Pradesh Panchayat Raj Act, 1994, introduced a new possibility for the rural poor to participate in grassroots politics because of reservation. Here was an opportunity to challenge the power of the landowning rich to take over Panchayats which had hitherto been controlled by the Reddys and the Kammas.

If there was any historical opportunity for the poor to come into politics it was in 1995 when elections were held for the first time under the new A.P. Panchayat Raj Act which reserved more than 60 per cent seats of Sarpanches and Ward members for SC, ST, BC and women.

In addition, the Gram Panchayat elections were declared to be non-party, i.e., no party symbol could be used. YIP saw in these elections a tremendous opportunity for the members of the unions that the YIP had been organising to contest for power.

YIP's IDEOLOGY AND WORK

Young India Project, a federation of 20 activist groups working in A.P., has been organising unions of the rural poor in six districts: Anantapur, Chittoor, Nellore, Kurnool, Cuddapah and Nalgonda. The members of the union cut across caste, gender and religious lines. Of the total members, 46 per cent are women. As far as caste-wise distribution is concerned, 50 per cent are SCs and STs, 40 per cent are BCs and 10 per cent poor minorities and other castes.

By March 31st, 1995, unions had been formed in 132 Mandals and the total membership stood at 265,526, of them 120,946 being women. These unions had been taking up struggles on land[2], house sites, bank loans, saving and DWCRA, community facilities such as drinking water, road construction, electricity extension, etc., and atrocities on SCs, STs and women.

The fact that all castes and religions were represented in the union and nearly 50 per cent of the union members were women made the Mandal level union an ideal secular body to contest in Panchayat Raj elections as an organisation representing all the poor in the Panchayat. The YIP realised the potential of the union to enable the rural poor to participate in Panchayat elections as members of an organised body, very much like the rich participate in the elections as members of a political party.

The YIP believes that social transformation of Bourgeois Democracy, which, in India, is really an elected oligarchy (government of the rich), cannot come about except through the struggles of the classes and gender which have been marginalised economically, socially and politically by the richer classes (Bedi 1997).

It must be noted, however, that the model for transformation offered by the Leninist and Stalinist ideology through the capture of state power by the Communist Party is not relevant in the existing Indian situation.

As far back as 1986, the YIP had separated from the communist line and had, in its place, accepted the strategy of a permanent struggle against capitalism to transform it to socialism, and the YIP also came to believe that, in this struggle, the rural poor masses were the main force of transformation. The YIP and other like-minded NGOs were supporters of the struggle. The support was provided in the form of ideological inputs, organisational inputs and finally, coordination and guidance of the struggles taken up by the masses.

By the end of 1994, the YIP was convinced that Panchayat Raj elections should become a major issue for struggle by the rural poor using reservations to their advantage. The YIP groups decided to educate and organise the rural people in all the 132

Mandals to participate in the Panchayat Raj elections which were to be held in 1995 in Andhra Pradesh.

YIP's PRE-ELECTION CAMPAIGN

Realising that the rural poor had never contested Panchayat Raj elections either as Sarpanches or as Ward members on their own volition, it was felt by all YIP leaders that first a massive training should be given to union leaders to make them understand how reservations could be used to their advantage, and, if elected, how they could use their new found powers to implement the development programmes to their advantage.

The YIP issued a paper titled "The Panchayat System: A Brief Historical Analysis" (Bedi 1994). It also compiled and published a booklet in Telugu called, "A.P. Panchayat Raj Act, 1994: Simplified and Explained selectively for Agricultural Labour Unions" (YIP 1994). Using these two documents and with the help of CAPART which gave the YIP Rs. 195,360, seven training programmes were conducted in six districts. The subjects covered in these three-day training programmes were: (1) History of Panchayat Raj Institutions; (2) A.P. Panchayat Raj Act of 1994; and (3) Planning and Campaigning for Panchayat Raj Elections.

In total, 1,080 union members were trained; of them, 432 were women and 500 belonged to the categories of SCs and STs. The training programmes were conducted between 21st September and 10th December, 1994. The last day of the training was spent on developing a strategy for contesting and campaigning for the elections. The strategy included formation of Mandal level election committees, selection of candidates and formulation of a manifesto for elections.

Along with the training, a movie was produced on how to contest in the coming elections and this was shown in all the Panchayats where there were strong unions.

Lastly, in each district, the YIP groups helped Mandal unions to prepare street plays and songs on Panchayat elections. Nothing was left to chance; before the elections in June, all the details relating to planning and organisation were completed.

ELECTION STRATEGIES

Under the new Act, elections to Zilla and Mandal Parishads were to be held under party banners; but elections to the Gram Panchayat were to be on non-party basis.

As this was the first time that the union members were participating in the Panchayat elections, a decision was taken by the YIP leaders to advise the unions not to participate in Zilla and Mandal elections because they were to be conducted on party basis. The unions, therefore, did not field any candidate for Zilla and Mandal elections. But, in spite of that, many members decided to participate as individuals with party and union support. At the end, 114 union members were elected as Mandal Parishad Representatives (MPR). Later, the YIP realised that it was an error to have advised the unions not to participate in Zilla and Mandal Parishad elections.

For the Gram Panchayat elections, an election strategy was evolved. Under the election strategy, the Mandal level committee of each union was advised and guided to select Panchayats to contest where membership was the highest. A strategy was also worked out to select candidates for reserved seats with participation of all the community members of the castes for which the seats were reserved. If there were two seats reserved for SCs, and not all the SC families were members of the union, then a deal was negotiated wherein one candidate was selected from among the non-union families, and one member from the union families. The agreement being that the union would vote for the non-union candidate and the non-union members would vote for the union candidate in case of third or a fourth member also deciding to contest with the support of the landed classes. This understanding was arrived at with SC, ST, BC and minority communities.

In some Panchayats, where Congress candidates were strong, the union made an alliance with the TDP to get its members elected. In those Panchayats where TDP was strong, alliances were formed with the Congress party.

The selection of candidates for Ward and Sarpanch seats, and the alliance/understanding to be arrived at, were left to the Mandal level committee because they best understood the power relations at the local level. The strategy paid rich dividends.

In all the six districts, 7,326 union members contested for Ward seats. Of them, 5,620 (i.e., 77 per cent) were victorious. Out of 5,620 winning candidates, 1,795 were women. Of 575 union members contesting for Sarpanch seats, 511 won; of them, 176 were women. In total, 7,901 union members were victorious primarily because of reservation and the election strategies adopted.

These overall statistics do not give an idea of the problems and the opposition the candidates of the unions had to face from the landed classes who resented the participation of SC, ST, BC and specially women in the elections without seeking their approval or support. This was a clear challenge to the traditional power exercised by them. Selected case studies are presented in Boxes 8.1 and 8.2 for further information.

BOX 8.1 : GUMMAKONDA PANCHAYAT

The total population in Gummakonda Panchayat of Dhone Mandal in Kurnool district is 1,445; of them, the male population is 734 and female population 711. The post of Sarpanch is reserved for SC woman. Out of eight wards in the Gram Panchayat, three are reserved for SC community and another three for BC community. The YIP union has a membership of 180 in this Gram Panchayat. Out of six ward positions reserved for SC and BC, the union won three seats. The union member also contested for the position of Sarpanch.

Against the union supported candidate of a SC woman for Sarpanch post, the leader Ramaswamy put up an illiterate SC woman as TDP supported candidate. He went to the SC colony two days before the elections along with the TDP goondas and told the union members not to cast any vote for the union candidate.

Some of the SC youth who were present said they would vote for the union candidate; they were beaten. On the day of the election, Ramaswamy's goondas stood by the SC colony and threatened to beat anyone who would go to vote.

The union candidate lost by 45 votes. The union filed a case against Ramaswamy under the A.P. Panchayat Raj Act. The case is still going on.

BOX 8.2 : MUKTHAPURAM PANCHAYAT

The Gram Panchayat of Mukthapuram in Mudigubba Mandal of Anantapur district has 6 villages in its jurisdiction. Out of total population of 4,520, the union has a membership of 600. The Sarpanch post was reserved for BC community.

The Union Secretary, Mr. Narayana, contested for the post of Sarpanch but lost by a margin of 279 votes. A total of 5 candidates stood for this election. The union candidates had the second highest votes polled. The upper caste members had selected their own illiterate BC person to serve their purpose.

During the campaign the upper caste members sent a letter to the union candidate threatening his life if he did not withdraw from the contest. The union members used this letter as propaganda to expose the upper caste members. Further, violence was threatened against the union members; but, the union decided to take up the challenge and contest for the Sarpanch post.

On the day of election, the upper caste members finding that the union members were able to gather in large numbers in support of thc union candidate, got some goondas and their supporters from the surrounding villages. With this force, they captured the booths and indulged in rigging. The union candidate lost because of this.

POST-ELECTION STRATEGY

Immediately after the elections, the YIP leaders from all the districts reviewed the election results and discussed what was to be done next. The first point that was expressed by all the leaders was that 90 per cent of the elected union members had no prior experience in Gram Panchayat management and, therefore, training was necessary. A second manual titled as 'How to run a Gram Panchayat' was prepared, and this was translated into Telugu.

The main topics covered were the role of Gram Panchayat in development, how development funds would be channelled from Zilla Parishad to the Gram Panchayat, the decision-making process in a Gram Panchayat and rules and regulations concerning meetings, responsibilities, use of funds, etc. Altogether, 8,000 such booklets were printed. The CAPART again came to the YIP's assistance and sanctioned Rs. 310,500 to train Sarpanches and Ward members who had contested on behalf of the unions and won.

Between 16th September and 11th November, 1995, seven two-day training programmes were organised for 549 male Sarpanches, 172 women Sarpanches and 321 union paid secretaries in how to run a Gram Panchayat. Subsequently, 80 one-day training programmes for Ward members were conducted in 128 Mandals. In these training programmes, 4,848 males and 1,790 women Ward members participated. In addition, 1,555 non-elected union members also attended the training programmes. In total, the YIP trained 9,237 members. Training programmes were completed by the end of 1995. We were optimistic that, with these training programmes, we would be able to show how well unions could run the Panchayats.

PROBLEMS

In January, 1995, even before the elections to the Panchayats took place, the TDP Government introduced Rs. 2.00 per kg. rice and prohibition. These two programmes alone cost the Government Rs. 2,500 crores annually. In the post-Panchayat Raj election period, the state was near bankruptcy and no funds were available for the development programmes. Under the Panchayat Raj Act, implementation of development programmes was the main function and the responsibility of PRIs, and the drying up of funds paralysed these institutions.

Throughout 1995-96, because of scarcity of funds in A.P., apart from limited JRY funds, Gram Panchayats received very little other funds for development. The YIP unions campaigned against Rs. 2.00 per kg. rice and prohibition. The former programme was subsequently modified, i.e., rice price was increased from Rs. 2.00 to Rs. 3.50 per kg. and the total prohibition was lifted by 31st March, 1997. May be in 1998, the financial situation of the A.P. Government will change and development funds will start flowing into Gram Panchayats.

The second problem the Gram Panchayats faced was that the cheque signing authority was not transferred from the previously appointed Sarpanches to the newly elected Sarpanches until a year after the elections. Even after the state government passed a G.O. giving the new elected Sarpanches and Group Executive Officer (GEO) cheque signing authority, the powerful Reddy and Kamma Sarpanches refused to hand over the accounts, the cheque books, and the Panchayat files to the new Sarpanches belonging to the SC, ST, BC communities. In most of the union Panchayats, the documents were demanded and received; but, in the non-union Panchayats the newly elected Sarpanches were too afraid to ask.

The third problem that the Gram Panchayats faced was the introduction of Prajala Vaddaku Palana (PVP) which was introduced by the Chief Minister, Mr. Chandrababu Naidu, on his coming to power in January, 1996. Under the PVP, a nodal officer was appointed for each Mandal and along with him or her, Mandal officials were required to visit each Gram Panchayat, hold meetings with all the members of the Panchayats inclusive of the elected Sarpanches and Ward members and make a list of works to be undertaken in the Gram Panchayat area under the PVP, with 50 per cent of the cost of the work being contributed by the members of the Gram Panchayat in the form of *shramadan* or free labour. The balance 50 per cent funds being released by the state as PVP funds.

This meant that development funds under the present government became PVP funds to be channelled not through the PRIs but through the official machinery. The powers and responsibilities that had been given to the grassroots elected leaders through the 73rd Amendment and the A.P. Panchayat Raj Act, 1994, were taken back by the present Government through the PVP.

Now, the Sarpanches and the GEOs have cheque signing authority, but, there are no funds in the Gram Panchayats for the Sarpanches and GEO to sign the cheque.

In addition, there is no point in holding the Panchayat meetings to make decisions on developmental programmes to be taken up within the Gram Panchayats because such decisions are taken not in Gram Panchayat meetings but in PVP meetings.

The YIP has issued a position paper on the PVP and *shramadan*, opposing both (YIP 1996). The YIP unions have agitated against the PVP and boycotted *shramadan* works. But, both the programmes continue because TDP is in power.

It is wondered whether in other states also ruling classes are ensuring in one way or another that grassroots democracy is not allowed to function. All the YIP's efforts and all the energy invested by the union members in Panchayat elections have been neutralised and nullified by the present TDP Government. The YIP unions have decided to take the TDP Government to the Supreme Court. Will that produce results?

Finally, it would be pertinent to mention another problem which surfaced during 1996 through a study conducted by Dr. Suvarchala on YIP's involvement in Panchayat elections in two Mandals of Andhra Pradesh; Somandepalli and Gummagatta[3].

She found that the one and two-day training conducted by the YIP for Sarpanches and Ward members had failed to produce the desired impact especially in the case of women. Even after the training, they allowed their husbands to attend and participate in Gram Panchayat meetings. What the YIP groups realised was that one day training by itself would not suffice, and that a long term follow-up strategy was also needed to enable SC, ST, BC and women elected under reservation to participate actively in Gram Panchayat meetings and decision-making.

Subsequently, it was decided that each Mandal leader-cum-union secretary must adopt 4 to 5 Gram Panchayats to do follow-up work which would include attending meetings, maintaining minutes and keeping record of developmental funds received by each adopted Gram Panchayat and how they have been utilised.

It will take a year or two of such follow-up work to develop confidence in the newly elected members so that they can play an effective role in Gram Panchayats.

FUTURE PLANS

In spite of all the problems, the YIP's belief that the poor must contest and capture Panchayat Raj power and use this power to their benefit has not diminished and will not diminish. The YIP is now working in 210 Mandals. The YIP's future plans are that YIP unions should capture at least 50 per cent of all Gram Panchayats in the 210 Mandals in the next Panchayat Raj elections which are scheduled to take place in the year 2000. In these elections, the YIP will encourage and guide the unions to even participate in Mandal and Zilla Parishad elections also.

To the YIP, the hope for the poor lies in their capacity to organise themselves to such an extent that they can challenge the ruling classes in the struggle for power in the PRIs. If they fail to make good in this challenge to the class which has enjoyed too much power for too long a time, the poor will remain where they are.

There is no alternative to a mass revolution from below and the YIP is committed to such a revolution. The question one can ask is, who are all willing to join the masses in this revolution. Are you?

NOTES

1. For details on the concept and its relation to PRIs, see, Bedi (1997).
2. For a detailed discussion on YIP's land struggles, see, Bedi (1996).
3. A few of the issues are covered in Suvarchala's paper in this volume.

REFERENCES

Bedi, Narinder (1994). *The Panchayat System: A Brief Historical Analysis.* Penukonda: Young India Project. Mimeo.

Bedi, Narinder (1996). Land to the Tiller: Peasant Struggles in Anantapur District. In B.N. Yugandhar (ed.), *Land Reforms in India: Andhra Pradesh—People's Pressure and Administrative Innovations.* New Delhi: Sage.

Bedi, Narinder (1997). PRIs and Social Transformation. In M.K. Bhat *et al.* (eds.), *Partners in Progress: Experiences of Voluntary Organisations in India*. Bangalore: DSI.

YIP (Young India Project) (1994). *A.P. Panchayat Raj Act, 1994: Simplified and Explained selectively for Agricultural Labour Unions*. Penukonda: Young India Project. Mimeo.

YIP (1995). *How to run a Gram Panchayat*. Penukonda: Young India Project. Mimeo.

YIP (1996). *A Position Paper on Prajala Vaddaku Palana (PVP) and Shramadan*. Penukonda: Young India Project. Mimeo.

9

SANGHAMITRA's INTERFACE WITH GRAM PANCHAYATS

K. SIVAJI

INTRODUCTION

Sanghamitra Service Society (hereinafter, Sanghamitra), registered under A.P. Societies Act of 1860, has been involved in development work since 1986. It works in Kanchikacherla, Veerulapadu, Vijayawada and Vungaturu Mandals of Krishna district, Andhra Pradesh. Sanghamitra has initiated various activities for the development of the down-trodden, especially women in 18 villages of these four Mandals. The organisation has also started a Destitute Women Rehabilitation Centre at Telaprulu village in Vungaturu Mandal of Krishna district and also works in an urban slum in Vijayawada.

The objectives of the organisation are: (i) to help and promote peaceful and constructive activities for socio-economic change; (ii) to undertake Gandhiji's constructive programmes; (iii) to promote people's organisations; and (iv) to promote income generation activities for the economic development of the rural poor women.

Some of the important activities initiated to translate these objectives are: (i) promotion of self-help groups and other organisations among the poor; (ii) initiating income generation programmes through savings and credit activities; (iii) enabling the people to have interface with government programmes; (iv) undertaking various training programmes; and (v) housing programme. Sanghamitra works with women from scheduled and backward castes, and minorities. Most of the target group members belong to landless agricultural labour category. There are 10 permanent and 15 temporary staff members working for the organisation.

By 1997, Sanghamitra had organised 175 self-help groups consisting of 2,095 members. These members saved over Rs. 2 lakhs and availed over Rs. 12.5 lakhs for various income generating programmes. In addition, women members also availed benefits from the government in the form of DWCRA loans, housing programme, etc.

Sanghamitra is of the opinion that interface with Gram Panchayats would help in realising the overall objective of the organisation. One of its objectives is to promote organisations among the poor. Sanghamitra believes that Gram Panchayat is also one of the well established, recognised and elected people's organisation. But when it comes to the implementation of the developmental activities and people's participation, the PRIs are not able to properly fulfil their responsibility because of the vested interests. The people, especially the poor, are also not aware of the functioning of the PRIs and they are also not trained in this regard. Social issues like caste, economic status, etc., are contributing to the lack of participation from the people. Sanghamitra believes that if PRIs are strengthened, and the poor are made to involve, then the role of vested interests would gradually weaken and pro-poor development can take place.

PRE-ELECTION STRATEGY

Thus, one of the objectives of Sanghamitra was to facilitate the participation of its target group members in Gram Panchayats. The issues such as the role of vested interests in Gram Panchayats and inability of the poor people to question the vested interests were always discussed in normal monthly meetings of the organisation before the 73rd Constitutional Amendment. When the elections to Gram Panchayats were announced in 1995, Sanghamitra started making sincere efforts to enable the target group to participate in the Gram Panchayats.

In order to prepare the target group to participate in local Gram Panchayats, the organisation itself needed to go through a preparatory process. As a part of this, Sanghamitra attended three training programmes: (i) a workshop organised by the Bhagavathula Charitable Trust (BCT); (ii) one day meeting with Mr. T.N. Seshan, the then Chief Election Commissioner; and, (iii) a training programme organised by the Gandhi Peace Centre (GPC), Hyderabad. By attending these workshops, the organisation became familiar with the strategies to be adopted before, during, and after the elections to Gram Panchayats. The meetings also inspired the organisation to initiate training programmes aimed at providing awareness on the functioning of Gram Panchayats under the new Constitutional Amendment and the importance of voters' education in this regard. The organisation was also enthused as it felt that there is now a good opportunity for the poor Dalit women, the people with whom the organisation is working, to enter into elected bodies at the grassroots level.

Sanghamitra, however, felt that there is a need to provide training to the leaders of Mahila Mandals who have potential to contest and win in the elections. The training programmes, conducted before the elections, were organised by both Sanghamitra and GPC.

Training programmes organised by Sanghamitra

Sanghamitra conducted four two-day training programmes for the leaders of Mahila Mandals. For these meetings, the boarding charges were borne by the organization, while travel expenses were borne by the participants. Topics covered in these training programmes were: (1) Panchayat Raj Act of Andhra Pradesh; (2) reservations for women and their potential benefits; (3) problems to be faced from local landlords, politicians, etc., during the elections; and, (4) how do rigging and other malpractices take place in the elections.

Training programmes organised by the GPC

The Women Resource Centre of GPC also provided two three-day training programmes for the leaders of Mahila Mandals. In these training programmes, emphasis was more on the relationship between people's organisations such as Mahila Mandals and Gram Panchayats before, during, and after the elections to Gram Panchayats. Other topics discussed were the resources at the disposal of Gram Panchayat, and how people's organisations should obtain information on the resources and prevent their mis-utilisation. The rights provided in the 73rd Constitutional Amendment for ordinary Ward members were also discussed in detail.

STRATEGY DURING THE ELECTIONS

After providing training to the leaders of Mahila Mandals, Sanghamitra facilitated a discussion among Mahila Mandal leaders on strategies to be employed during the elections. The organisation sought to educate the members of Mahila Mandals on how to select a candidate based on certain criteria such as sincerity and honesty, education, leadership qualities, capability to contest and win the elections, capacity to deliver goods after the elections. It was also suggested that a member who has comparative advantages should be selected. Subsequently, the Mahila Mandals themselves selected the candidates for the elections.

In all, 11 members of Mahila Mandals contested for Ward Membership; of them, eight got elected unanimously. Thus, in most of the cases, the candidates were elected unanimously. This was, because, the moment a candidate was selected by a Mahila Mandal, the other sections in the village did not want to put up any opposition candidate. In some cases, a possible contest was avoided by taking strategic decisions. For instance, in one of the villages, Mahila Mandals wanted to nominate Venkayamma as a Ward member. But, it came to know that Kammas, who form a majority, were keen that Chandravathi, also a Mahila Mandal member, should become Ward member. As Mahila Mandal members were indifferent between these two candidates, they took a decision to support the candidature of Chandravathi. This avoided a possible election and conflict between two members of Mahila Mandal.

Sanghamitra is aware of the fact that it did not facilitate any member to contest for Sarpanch's post. This was because of the target group approach that the organization is following. As the target group of Sanghamitra does not command a majority in the villages, any attempt to contest for the Sarpanch post was considered to be a futile exercise by Mahila Mandal members.

Sanghamitra provided moral support to the candidates. As a majority of the candidates stood for the elections for the first time, there was need to support and instil confidence in them. There was also need to look into the tendencies that force members to withdraw from the election process. It organised Mahila Mandal meetings before the elections to educate the members regarding prevention of clashes and cross voting.

POST-ELECTION STRATEGY

After the elections, Sanghamitra conducted training programmes for the elected members. In addition to eight elected members from its target group, 22 other members, who were friendly to Sanghamitra target group, were called for the training programmes. So far, the organisation has conducted three two-day training programmes for the elected members. The boarding expenditure was borne by the organisation, while the travel expenses were borne by the participants.

The aim of the training programmes was to build the skills and capacities of the elected members. The role of elected Ward members in Gram Panchayats was discussed in these training programmes. Some of the topics that were handled in the training programmes were: (i) the Gram Panchayat meetings, the need to attend all the meetings and questioning the Sarpanch, if meetings are not regularly conducted; (ii) the resources earmarked for development work at Gram Panchayat level and how the resources are to be utilised; (iii) the past tendencies with regard to utilising contractors in the implementation of development work and the need to question such practices; and, (iv) the past tendencies of mis-utilisation and diversion of development resources and the need to question them. It was also communicated that a Ward member should not simply sign in the register and that they need to actively participate in Gram Panchayat functioning.

These training programmes have had considerable impact on the functioning of Ward members in Gram Panchayat. The elected Ward members from Sanghamitra target group are raising several questions and are able to put pressure on the Sarpanches on the need to organise meetings regularly, preventing corruption and other malpractices, etc. In Kothapeta village, a women Ward member belonging to Sanghamitra complained to the Panchayat Raj Officer that signatures are being sought by the President without holding meetings. In several villages, the Ward members are giving information to the people about the resources that flowed into Gram Panchayat and the way they have been utilised.

At the same time, there are also problems. One elected woman Ward member is coopted by a political party. She, on her own, made efforts to obtain party positions after the elections. Of late, she is not sharing the information on resources flowing into Gram Panchayats and the way they have been utilised for development works with the members of Mahila Mandals. The Mahila Mandal members are of the opinion that she is becoming corrupt as she does not any more participate in agricultural coolie work. The members also complain that she often tells that 'I am responsible for that', 'I did that', etc., and does not acknowledge the role of Mahila Mandal members. The general impression is that she is not accountable to the people.

Two more elected members were also coopted by the political party. Unlike the previous case, these two members did not make any efforts to join the political party. But, political parties themselves nominated them for some party positions. They are still accountable to the people.

FUTURE PERSPECTIVES

The co-option of a few of the elected members into the political process and their lack of accountability to the Mahila Mandals is a cause of concern to Sanghamitra. On considerable introspection, the organisation realised that the participation of the target group in 1995 elections was not process oriented and that the organisation had committed strategic mistakes.

The first strategic mistake was concentration on a few leaders from each Mahila Mandal. In the past, all the training programmes were conducted for them, and only leaders participated in exposure trips. In a way, they became an extended arm of the organisation in the villages. It also appears that some of these leaders entertained political aspirations and that they were not accountable to the members in the past also.

Secondly, in the absence of capacity building of ordinary members, they are not able to question the attitude of some of the elected members. The organisation is, therefore, planning to improve the capacity of ordinary members in issues relating to Gram Panchayats. Mahila Mandal members can then contribute to make Gram Panchayats pro-poor organisations.

Thirdly, the organisation is planning to build a critical mass in the project area. Sanghamitra has been working with a fixed target group. It has now realised that it is very difficult for the poor Dalits to contest and capture Gram Panchayats if it works with only one section of the target group. In the last two years, self-help groups have been formed for those poor who were earlier not part of the Mahila Mandals. The plan is to gradually increase the number of target group members in each village and capture Gram Panchayats at the village level.

The organisation is also of the opinion that the preparation should not begin when the election process is about to be commenced. It has been making efforts for the last couple of years to prepare the people for the next elections which are scheduled to be held in 2000 A.D. As a part of this, training programmes are being regularly held, critical mass is being built up and legal aspects of Gram Panchayat are being carefully examined so that legal action could be taken up in the event of target group members of Sanghamitra not having a majority in a Gram Panchayat.

In the light of the above, the organisation realises that the training once or twice is not sufficient, and it should be regular. Based on the identified issues relating to the PRI, it is essential to find out the suitable resource persons and involve them in the training. Sanghamitra will have to look into the legal aspects of the PRI, and if there is need, efforts should be made to find ways and means of preparing the target groups to take up the legal action. These are some of the future perspectives which the organisation is thinking.

APPENDIX 9.1: A WOMAN MEMBER OF PARITALA GRAM PANCHAYAT

T. Padmavathi, a target group member of Sanghamitra, got elected to Paritala Gram Panchayat. Paritala is a revenue village in Kanchikacherla Mandal of Krishna District with a population of around 4,000. Of the total population, 2,000 members belong to the SC community, while around 500 members belong to the Muslim community. The remaining, largely belong to the categories of ST, BC and others. The Gram Panchayat consists of 14 elected members, of whom, 10 members belong to the SC community, 2 belong to the Muslim community and the remaining two belong to other communities. Three out of 14 seats are reserved for women. Unfortunately, the SC community, which holds a majority of votes in the village, was unable to win the Gram Panchayat Sarpanch post. This post was won by a person belonging to the other community by sheer muscle and money power.

Background of T. Padmavathi

Padmavathi is married and two of her daughters are also married and settled. In addition, her background is as follows:

* Runs a small tea centre for her day-to-day survival.
* Even before Gram Panchayat elections, she formed a Mahila Mandal in her village with the co-operation of Sanghamitra.
* She is the President of the Mahila Mandal in her village.
* Initiated thrift and economic activity among the group members.
* Attended the training programmes on leadership, motivation camps, and other relevant activities benefiting the Mahila Mandal organised by Sanghamitra.

* Even without an active support from Sanghamitra, she is able to interact with government agencies directly for mobilising resources for the Mahila Mandal.
* She is highly regarded by members in the Mahila Mandal.

Once the schedule for the Gram Panchayat elections was declared, the members of the Mahila Mandal pursued her to contest as a Ward member. She was elected unanimously from her Ward which was reserved for women. In the early stages, with her limited knowledge of the role and responsibility of Panchayat member, she was not able to play an active role in the Gram Panchayat meetings. During this phase, she was exposed to a training programme 'On Women's Role in Panchayat', which was organised by Sanghamitra. After attending the training programme, she did correct herself and started asserting herself in the Gram Panchayat meetings. She was able to raise her voice by putting questions on:

* funds allocation for the village and their proper utilisation;
* the poor quality of civil works; and
* diversion of funds allocated to the SC community for others.

The following is an example of her fight for the cause of the poor. The Housing Programme for the poor belonging to the SC community was sanctioned by the government. The Sarpanch of the Gram Panchayat with his political contacts at higher levels wanted to divert the funds meant for the SC community to strengthen his own political base. When this came to her notice, she protested at the Gram Panchayat meeting. She also met the government officials and the local MLA in this regard. She could convince them about the need to spend the funds earmarked for the SC community. She got back the funds which were in any case meant for the SC community. This made the Sarpanch very angry and also hurt his ego. The Sarpanch of the Gram Panchayat started creating problems to her to safeguard his own vested interests.

Now, even genuine protests are ignored in the Gram Panchayat meetings and there is absolutely no support either from women members or male members for her. In the meetings, resolutions are passed with the help of Sarpanch's own men who are the quorum in the Gram Panchayat. After undergoing this sort of an experience, she is now getting frustrated. She is in a dilemma, and asks the following question. Under these circumstances, what kind of role could I play to make the Gram Panchayat undertake the pro-poor developmental activities?

APPENDIX 9.2: A CASE OF A WOMAN WHO COULD NOT GET ELECTED

Perakalapadu is a small village in Kanchikacherla Mandal of Krishna District with a population of 1,500. Out of the total population, 800 were SC families, while 700 were BC families. The Gram Panchayat in this village consists of 8 elected members and the post of the Sarpanch is reserved for women. Two seats in the Gram Panchayat are also reserved for women.

Vedanki Devamma is the President of local Mahila Mandal where the main activities are thrift, credit and undertaking of economic programmes. She has a small grocery shop for her own sustenance. She actively participates in Sanghamitra's activities. Once the Panchayat election was announced, she filed her nomination for the post of Ward member. This village happens to be the birthplace of the local MLA. The local political leaders wanted some other dummy female candidate for the Ward membership for their own political and financial gains, and hence, wanted Devamma to withdraw. The reasons why the local leaders wanted her to withdraw are:

1. she is vociferous;
2. she has skills of organisation which she developed as the President of the Mahila Mandal; and
3. she has a tendency to question others.

With these qualities the local leaders thought that she will be a hurdle in obtaining political gains and may contribute to the erosion of their political base. Hence, the local leaders pressurised her to withdraw. They also threatened her with serious consequences if she did not withdraw. Lastly, the local MLA intervened and made her to withdraw from contesting in the elections. The local MLA and the other local political leaders made a weak, voiceless and dummy female as the Ward member.

After all this, the local leaders are still playing their own games in the activities relating to her Mahila Mandal. DWCRA was sanctioned by the government for the group. The local political leaders tried to stall the sanctioning of the programme to the members of the Mahila Mandal. They made the group to visit the relevant government department for a number of times. The money for DWCRA programme was released after a considerable delay. Her main question is that 'in this kind of system, what kind of an active role can I play for the betterment of the oppressed poor?'

10

EXPERIENCES OF 'SHARE' IN ITS ATTEMPT AT ENSURING PARTICIPATION OF WOMEN IN THE ELECTION TO LOCAL ADMINISTRATION

K. Murugesan

INTRODUCTION

Self-help Association for Rural Education and Employment (SHARE) is a membership based women's organisation registered under Tamil Nadu Societies Act. SHARE works in 27 villages in Kaniambadi block of Vellore taluk, Vellore district of Tamil Nadu. This block is located 140 kms. away from Chennai. The total population in 27 villages is approximately 79,000, of whom 50 per cent are women. SHARE works with 6,000 women who mainly belong to landless and marginal farmer families. Frequent failures of monsoons, lack of irrigation and employment opportunities are some of the major problems in the area. The main sources of employment are agriculture, construction, stone cutting, brick making, etc. The wages earned by women from agricultural work range from Rs. 20 to Rs. 25 per day. The literacy rate among women is low and drop-out rate is high. Women have very little freedom and have no say in decision-making either at home or outside.

Ever since its formation in 1992, SHARE[1] has been putting efforts to bring about all-round development of its members and member families. The main objective of the organisation is 'total empowerment of the poor through income generating programmes'. The important activities are: (i) enabling the poor to undertake income generating activities through skill upgradation, marketing and raw material support;[2] and (ii) providing education and support services for the poor and their children[3]. Besides contributing to an improvement in family income[4] and thereby improve the health status of member families, SHARE has also been taking up programmes and activities aimed at bringing about social change.

Awareness programmes on matters relating to the development of women, equality of women, women's rights in family and society, etc., combined with training programmes on the development of leadership skills and personality improvement have helped these women to move a step forward on the road to empowerment which is the ultimate goal of SHARE.

As a membership based women's organisation, SHARE has undertaken all its activities and programmes paying due respect to the total participation, and adoption of this policy has imbibed continuous interest and raised the level of motivation of all its members, the executive and the staff (Bickel 1997).

Apart from undertaking programmes meant for the development of its members and their families, SHARE has always felt that it has a commitment to the community at large and this realisation has guided SHARE to initiate some community welfare activities which include the introduction of group life insurance scheme, a scholarship scheme for girl students, the arrangement for an individual and family counselling programme, etc.

But, SHARE keeps asking itself the following questions: Is it enough for SHARE to confine itself to activities and programmes relating to income generation and welfare? Is it not necessary for SHARE to widen its area of operation to encompass issues and matters that will be helpful in the long run to make it possible for women to increase their level of participation in decision-making at the community level? If at all this becomes necessary, what role can SHARE play in making this possible?

The above questions have been argued at length in several forums and the answer that came out during all these deliberations is that SHARE needs to play an active role and this has been translated into action.

The following is an account of SHARE's involvement in the elections to PRIs. An attempt has been made here to describe why and how the decision was taken, what pre-poll activities were undertaken and with what results, how did the women contestants fared in the elections, when failed what were the reasons for the failures, what is the post-election scenario, etc.

PRE-ELECTION STRATEGY

Even as the Central government was seriously considering reservations for women in elections to the local administrative bodies, the SHARE started earnestly discussing the need for undertaking the responsibility of providing its members with complete knowledge about the new PRIs and also motivate at least a handful of them to contest if and when elections were announced and held at a future date[5]. The SHARE believed that skills provided to several of its members through a series of leadership training programmes should enable them to meet the demands of leading local communities for their all-round development. Having resolved to take up a programme to this end, SHARE was looking for an agency that would come forward to sponsor an education programme to its members and also the general public.

Towards the end of 1995, GTZ/SHF provided financial assistance for the project entitled, 'Improvement of Socio-Economic Conditions of Women'. One of the several components of this project was the creation of awareness about the new Panchayat Raj system. With funds made available, SHARE was able to undertake the programme in right earnest, and following is the description of the various aspects of this awareness programme and the experiences acquired thereof.

Aims and objectives of the Panchayat Raj awareness programmes

SHARE had set the following objectives in undertaking the Awareness Programmes about the new Panchayat Raj system:

(i) Overall objective

* Women should become aware of their rights, in general, and with special regard to PRIs, in particular.

(ii) Specific objectives

* Members of SHARE should participate in local Panchayat elections when held.
* At least three villages in SHARE's project area should have active women members in Panchayats.

Activities undertaken

Towards the fulfilment of the above objectives, the following programmes were undertaken:

(i) Training programme for Animators

To begin with, it was felt necessary to organise an intensive training programme for a group of women who can subsequently act as resource persons at the community level and spread the knowledge about the new Panchayat Raj system introduced by the Central government. It was also expected that some among this group will ultimately be motivated to contest for various positions in the local bodies.

Accordingly, a training programme was organised for 30 persons who were working as animators in the craft centres of SHARE.

The topics taken up for discussion included women's rights, the old system of Panchayat administration, the newly announced Panchayat Raj system, motivational aspects, leadership style and functioning, etc. Experts[6] in conducting training programmes for grassroots level staff and workers were invited to organise and conduct the training programme.

The chief functionaries of SHARE also contributed to the training programme as they had already gained much knowledge about the subject through the training programmes organised by the Panchayat union at the block level for selected persons on constitutional provisions, training programme organised by South Indian Producer Associations (SIPA), Madras, and training programme organised by the Legal Resource for Social Action (LRSA), Chengalpet.

Books, manuals, video films produced by the LRSA were used as the resource material. Participatory discussions and role plays were the methods used to provide knowledge. As far as possible, lectures were avoided.

(ii) Awareness programme for the general public

Using the animators, four public awareness campaigns were organised, two in SHARE complex, and the others in Mothupalayam and Sholavaram villages. Apart from craft workers, men and women from other villages also participated in these programmes. Animators and craft workers who were tuned to the programmes provided advance publicity to the programmes and motivated village women to participate. Each of these four programmes was attended by more than 400 women and men.

Resource persons who conducted the training programme for the animators were invited to conduct these awareness programmes also. In these awareness programmes also, lectures were kept to the necessary minimum, and discussions and role plays were used to impart knowledge. The trained animators were used to put up role plays.

Impact of the training and awareness programmes

The effect of the training programme for the animators and subsequent awareness programmes for the craft workers and general public needs to be assessed on the basis of the stipulated objectives. With this in mind, a mid-term evaluation was organised by SHARE, inviting an outsider to complete the job[7]. The brief summary of the findings of the mid-term evaluation is presented hereunder:

(i) Mid-term evaluation on training programme for Animators

Seven of the 30 animators who attended the training programme were interviewed in a group. A predetermined schedule was used during the interview and the responses were recorded in a cassette player and as well manually by a recorder.

It was noticed that there was increase in knowledge, motivation and confidence levels of animators after the training.

* They knew about the power of the Gram Sabha.
* They knew that one-third seats have been reserved for women.
* They were confident that they will be able to motivate women in their villages to contest both for Ward membership and presidentship with or without the approval of their husbands and families.
* All of them believed that women can do things rightly and in a better way.
* They were in a position to find fault with the reservation policy, stating that the proportion of seats reserved for women should have been 50 per cent and not 33 per cent.

The impression gained by the evaluator was that quite a few will ultimately contest for Presidentship and Ward membership when elections were held.

(ii) Mid-term evaluation on awareness programmes for the general public

A group interview was organised for 10 women selected randomly using the lottery method out of a list of 70 persons who were known to have participated in the awareness programme. The findings were:

* most of them knew about the number of ballot papers that each voter has to cast;
* all of them knew about the appealing procedure to the Collector for the withdrawal of an erring Sarpanch or member; and
* most of them felt that it should be possible for them to find and motivate suitable women for Ward membership and Presidentship.

KNOWLEDGE INTO ACTION: STRATEGY DURING ELECTIONS

Whereas the knowledge, attitude and confidence levels were found to have increased because of the training and awareness programmes, the real impact could only be assessed at the performance level. Altogether, 13 women stood for Ward membership and three women for Presidentship in the recently concluded elections to the Panchayats. Of the 13 women who contested for Ward membership, five won the elections. Unfortunately, all the three women who stood for Presidentship did not win (Appendix 10.1). But, all of them had made a definite impression on the public, in general, and particularly, on women. It should be stated here that all of them had participated either in the Animator's Training Programme or Awareness Programme for the general public. Besides these women contestants, 7 youth (men) also stood for Ward membership and 6 of them won who were motivated by women.

Analysis of participation in elections

A post-mortem analysis of this exercise of making motivated and knowledgeable women participate in elections to the local bodies has revealed the following findings:

* All of them contested the elections as independent candidates. When it came to the question of contesting with candidates who had party affiliations, the exercise became too difficult.
* All of them were putting forth only their motivation, selflessness and concern for the community to canvass for votes. But, the common man in the villages opted to vote for candidates who paid money and supplied liquor (Appendix 10.1).
* In some cases, even though the women were motivated and prepared to participate in the elections to the PRI, they did not get the wholehearted support from their husbands/parents/families.
* Under the new system for election to the PRI, a person has to vote for 4 candidates. In some Wards, a voter has to vote

to select two Ward members. All these had created confusion among voters and led to increased percentage of invalid votes.

* The common man was unaware of the rules and regulations of this system. More than this, the officials themselves did not seem to have complete knowledge and skills in handling the affairs.
* One common observation was that the Returning Officer and his team members allowed themselves to be entertained by influential politicians and this adversely affected the morale of the women contestants. This had also led them to believe that these officials would in some way or the other be taking sides with the party candidate.
* In the case of two Panchayats, the women candidates of SHARE were contesting for Presidentship against the candidates put up by the village leadership. In both the cases, the women chose to oppose the village leadership on the ground that their candidates were inefficient, incapable of shouldering the responsibility of leading the community and who will always be needing their male counterparts to operate on their behalf (Appendix 10.1).
* In some cases, the contestants were overenthusiastic to fight the elections and two or three persons stood in the same Ward. Even though there was no direct confrontation between them, they lost the ground as the votes got split.
* There are instances when the community leaders themselves had persuaded the women to contest, placing complete faith in their efficiency and selflessness. These candidates did not have to spend anything apart from the deposit money and expenses of printing notices (Appendix 10.2).

FUTURE PERSPECTIVE

Winners as well as losers still wear a cheerful look. For them, having contested the elections in itself is considered to be a great achievement. Their participation in the elections has sent the signals to the local communities (especially the power mongers in these communities) that they are a force to reckon with from now on. Sooner or later, people are going to find fault with themselves for not having voted these women in places where they had waged a losing battle. Some people have started expressing it.

Procedural mistakes have also been observed: showing the signatures of Ward members for the meetings that were not held; and husbands leading the discussions in the meetings in the case of Panchayats which have women Presidents and also in the case of Panchayat Union which has a woman Chairperson.

SHARE women believe that preparation for future elections should begin from now on. This, they believe, can be done by working through the Ward members—guiding them to participate in the meetings and representing their area problems and grievances and by continuously engaging themselves in welfare and development activities as individuals and as groups.

SHARE has already been contemplating in terms of organising follow-up education programmes for the ward members and also the animators to guide them to function effectively as Ward members and as dutiful citizens.

SHARE has been nominated as a Block Level Advisory Development committee member and as an Advisory committee member at the district level by the local Administration. This would help SHARE to have a strong link with the PRIs in the district.

CONCLUSIONS

Two important questions need to be discussed: If the motivated women win the elections and become Sarpanches and members, the community will definitely benefit. But, contesting the elections and winning them means contending against money power. Should it mean that they should also spend money and win votes and elections?

Secondly, it has been found that due to various reasons which include close family relationship, inefficient and incompetent persons are chosen by the village leaders (especially in the case of those villages where seats are reserved for Scheduled

Caste). Should motivated and efficient women who can manage the affairs of the Panchayats contest against candidates proposed by the leaders in these places?

Notwithstanding these questions, a beginning has been made by SHARE. People in the villages of Kaniambadi have been given to understand that there is an organisation of women in their midst which will do everything to protect the interests of people in general and more particularly of women. On its part, SHARE will make its presence felt by continuing to take keen interest in the proper organisation and conduct of programmes and activities carried on through the PRIs and by establishing renewed contacts and relationship with the officials of the institutions and with the elected representatives of the people.

APPENDIX 10.1: CASE STUDY OF AN UNSUCCESSFUL CANDIDATE

Thuthipet Panchayat in Kaniambadi Block is a reserve constituency for women from the SCs. Besides SCs, the village is inhabited by Reddiars, a dominant caste group and Yadavas. Sirukalambur is the only hamlet of this Panchayat. In the recent past, some families from Thuthipet have moved to a place near the main road which lies at half a kilometre from the original village. Some people from outside the village also have built their houses there and are living there. This settlement also comes under Thuthipet Panchayat.

Sathiavani, an unsuccessful candidate, lives with her husband and children in this new habitat. She was born in Thuthipet colony and all her relatives continue to live there. Before marriage, she was working as a Balwadi teacher in a neighbouring village. She was married off to a person in a distant village. Her married life was not all that happy for her husband was a drunkard and a spendthrift. The tussles with in-laws almost broke the family. But, Sathiavani persuaded her husband to shift the family to the village where she was working as a Balwadi teacher before she got married. The management of the Balwadi had no hesitation in employing her once again. Having regained her job and rightful position in the family, she had no difficulty in managing her husband and her married life at last began to yield satisfaction and happiness. After some time, they found a place in the present hamlet and are living there since five years.

Announcement of the election and the aftermath

As a Balwadi teacher, Sathiavani was caring, able and looked after the children admirably. However, for reasons beyond control, the management closed the Balwadi. Sathiavani did not lose hope. She took to SHARE's palm leaf craft which she had learnt before and she did not lag behind others in this new venture. It was here that she acquired complete knowledge about the new PRIs. During the training, she decided to contest in the elections as and when they were announced.

Sathiavani decided to stand for the position of councillorship. SHARE also approved of her decision. But, things simply went wrong. Jaya, wife of Palani, an extension worker working with the Community Health and Development programme (CHAD), Christian Medical College (CMC), also wanted to contest in the elections. As an extension worker, Palani had done good work in the community. Jaya is a housewife and manages a petty shop. She has very little experience of the outside world and as such needed the continued assistance and help from her husband in case she became successful in the elections, whereas Sathiavani could hope to function independently and also effectively. In any case, there was no problem as Jaya wanted to contest for presidentship and Sathiavani for councillorship. Indeed that was the intention of both.

When SHARE was approached by Palani and his friends from the village, a lengthy discussion took place in the presence of Sathiavani. It was decided that there should be no contest between Sathiavani and Jaya as the former would contest for councillorship and the latter for presidentship.

After both the parties went back to Thuthipet, during that night the village elders[8] organised a meeting to decide the candidate. Sathiavani was not invited for this meeting whereas Jaya and

Palani were invited. When Sathiavani came to know of this, she felt offended, but she made it a point to reach the meeting place.

In the meeting, all the people unanimously nominated Jaya for presidentship. But, there was no mention of the nomination of Sathiavani for councillorship and this was in total violation of their agreement at the SHARE meeting. Sathiavani did not quite understand what had gone wrong. She tried to question first about not extending the invitation to her to attend the meeting. Then she questioned about the promise they had made. She was startled when she was told that she did not belong to the village and cannot hope to get their approval to contest in the elections. She tried to argue with them that her house and the new hamlet did come under the area of Thuthipet Panchayat and that she had been living there for five full years. But, all her arguments were of no avail. Drunken as they were, the language they used cannot be described here as they were long and filthy.

Sathiavani was enraged after finding that she had been cheated and humiliated. More than this what she could not bear was the statement that she did not belong to the village. This was denying her basic democratic rights. She decided that after all this, she should contest not for councillorship but for presidentship. No amount of persuasion by SHARE could change her stand.

The Election

Sathiavani waged a losing battle. In spite of her best efforts, she could get only 240 votes as against 600 by her principal opponent Jaya. The battle was virtually between Sathiavani and the others—Jaya, Palani and the village headman. Sathiavani believed in door to door canvassing only. She did not spend any money in electioneering. Even if she had wanted to, she had no money at her disposal. On the other hand, her opponent had apparently spent money especially to buy liquor.

Sathiavani has not developed any ill-will towards Jaya or Palani. Indeed, Sathiavani and Palani are very closely related to each other. She also believes that Palani will try his level best to do good to the people. But, her doubt is about Jaya functioning independently. She thinks that Jaya will function only through her husband in the front for everything. In that case, what will happen to women empowerment?

Sathiavani says that she might have lost the elections, but she has proved to Thuthipet people that she is not an outsider but belongs to the village very much. She wanted to prove it and she believes that she did it beyond doubt.

Inferences

If only the village leaders had been wise enough to keep to their original promises, Jaya could have become successful without spending any money and Sathiavani could have emerged successful as a councillor. Now that this confrontation had taken place between two persons from the same village, the village leaders have forfeited their claim to the councillorship which went to the neighbouring Panchayat. In the process, excepting the creation of enmity between two sections of the population, the village has not gained much.

APPENDIX 10.2: CASE STUDY OF A SUCCESSFUL CANDIDATE

Mothakkal village is the last village in the south-eastern direction of Kaniambadi Block. The total population of the village is 1,500, of which more than half live in field huts. Almost all of them belong to the Vanniya community, which is the dominant community in this Block.

CHAD has been catering to the health needs of this village through its part-time community health workers programme. CHAD had also organised a women's club in the village through which health and social problems were taken up for discussion in the monthly meetings. Non-formal and adult education centres also were started in the village to achieve 100 per cent literacy. The women's club activities motivated the young men of the village to come together to form a youth club. Through the women's club, a threshing platform was contributed with the help of CHAD, and a craft centre in palm leaf work was set up with SHARE's assistance.

Sengothai, about 38 years, and a married woman was behind all these developments. From the time the women's club was formed, Sengothai started associating herself in all its activities. She served as the President of this club for many years, and as the animator of the non-formal education centre. In all capacities, she had discharged her duties always putting the interest and welfare of the community first. Her husband is a drunkard and would create problems for her every now and then. But, Sengothai was able to overcome this problem mainly because she had developed her skills in communication to an extent that she would convince her husband that whatever she did will give unforeseen rewards. Sengothai belongs to the just above the poverty line group.

Even though Sengothai had attended the training programme organised by SHARE, she had no inclination to contest the elections. But, when the question of proposing some woman to contest for Ward position came, the village youth and leaders felt that Sengothai was the automatic choice and even without taking her consent filed the nomination paper. When Sengothai was told about this, she was confused. She had not consulted her drunkard husband and mother-in-law. What would be their reaction? The villagers who met her were confident about convincing the husband and the mother-in-law and they did it successfully.

What efforts did Sengothai make to canvass the votes? Nothing. She went with the contestant for presidentship to canvass votes for her. But even during these visits she personally did not ask anybody to vote for her. Did she print notices or posters? No. She did not spend any money on this. How did then people know about her symbol? From the notices and posters printed for presidentship that the people came to know about her symbol. Did anybody contest against her? Yes. Four persons. What was the outcome? She came off with flying colours. Out of 201 votes polled in the Ward, she collected as many as 129 votes.

Afterwards, there was a move from all quarters that she should be given the vice-presidentship. But this move was withdrawn, for the councillor and the president were also women. It was also felt that the vice-presidentship at least be given to a man.

What is her reaction about all that has happened? Even in the absence of any position or power she was contributing to the development of the village. Now that the people had further confided faith in her by electing her to an official position, she is very happy and at the same time feels more responsible in discharging her duties.

Apart from giving the opportunity to Sengothai to receive the benefit of the training programme, SHARE had not in any other way helped her in the electioneering. Indeed, as the community had decided in her favour, her success in the election was a foregone conclusion and there was no need for the members of SHARE to go with her for door to door canvassing which they had resorted to in other places.

NOTES

1. For a more detailed account on the evolution of SHARE, see, Rajamma and Nadarajan (1997), Raj (1995) and Murthi (1995).
2. SHARE initiated income earning opportunities like palm leaf craft, sisal fibre craft, korai mat weaving, etc. SHARE provides raw materials and sells the finished products in the national and international markets (Raj 1995). In 1995-96, products worth Rs. 30.53 lakhs were sold; of which, 99 per cent sold in the foreign market (Rajamma and Nadarajan 1997).
3. These include evening study centres and providing drinking water facilities.
4. Six hundred women workers in SHARE craft centres earned a profit of Rs. 1,079,962 in 1995-96 (Rajamma and Nadarajan 1997; 9). A study of sample beneficiaries at two points in time revealed that incomes increased by 30 to 50 per cent (Maruthamuthu 1997).
5. See, *The Hindu* (1996).
6. To Mention some of the resource persons: Prof. Rathna Natarajan, Tirupathur; Prof. Senthil Adhiban, Madras University; Miss Karpagam, Pudhu Vazhvu Maiyam, Vellore; Mr. Pushparaj, Director, Women Development Society, Vellore; Mr. Sivashanmugam, Health Educator, CHAD, CMC, Vellore; Mr. Maniraj, LRSA, Chengalpet; Mr. Pothireddy, Rtd. Jt. Registrar of Co-operatives, Madurai; and Mrs. Vatchala Siddharthan, Vellore.
7. See report by Maruthamuthu (1996).
8. In all the Harijan colonies, there is a Headman called Nattanmikarar and a few of his colleagues who, between them, form the traditional leadership of the group.

REFERENCES

Bickel, Amanda S. (1997). *Commerce with Cause? NGO and Cooperative Income Generation Projects in Three South Indian Villages.* Master's Thesis submitted to Massachusetts Institute of Technology, U.S.A.

Maruthamuthu, M. (1997). *SHARE: GTZ/SHF sponsored Self-Evaluation Report.* Vellore: SHARE. (Mimeo).

Murthi, P.V.V. (1995). Making Rural Women Self-reliant. *The Hindu,* October 16.

Raj, J.E. (1995). A Success Story that is Worth Sharing. *Exchanges*, 9.

Rajamma, G. and V.C. Nadarajan (1997). *Mid-Term Review of SHARE's Activities.* Vellore: SHARE. Mimeo.

The Hindu (1996). Village Women eager to Contest Panchayat Elections. *The Hindu.* March 8.

11

ROAD's PEOPLE BOUND JOURNEY

Mohammed Usman

INTRODUCTION

Rural Organisation for Action and Development (ROAD) started its 'People bound Journey' in 1977. Ever since, ROAD has placed its trust in people's abilities to develop themselves through their own empowerment, however weak and oppressed they are.

ROAD is functioning in about 46 villages in Shoolagiri and Veppanapalli Blocks of Dharmapuri District in Tamil Nadu, mostly among women through their Sanghas. Almost all the women of the Sanghas are engaged in dry land agriculture and belong to Dalits as well as other castes. In a number of villages, the membership is mixed. ROAD has a team of about 17 workers, and about 14 volunteers in the mass programme on functional literacy on part-time basis.

ROAD's main objectives are: 'help them who suffer the most' and 'empower them to empower themselves and others'. The activities initiated to realise the above objectives are: (i) community organisations/HRD training for empowerment; (ii) watershed and sustainable agricultural development; and (iii) on farm and off farm income generation activities. The strong belief of the organisation is that awareness education should precede any other development input or programmes. In those villages where awareness/education cannot proceed, it must, at least, go along with other programmes.

Empowerment process, as is well known, has several facets and this is not mere economic empowerment though this, in itself, is not unimportant. ROAD came across many examples of working and earning women suffering just because they are women. It is common knowledge that, in a majority of the cases, money earned is not under their own control. In rural areas and slums of the cities, their hard earned money is often spent on alcohol, gambling and otherwise, by their spouses. It is known that in many cases women do not (or not allowed to) have rights over their own body and health.

Political empowerment is another important facet which seems to ensure the empowerment for women in real terms. Political empowerment leads to self governance of women. In other words, politically empowered women are in a better position to have command over resources and other structures prevailing in the society. Wherever possible, women, therefore, need to enter into the positions of decision-making.

With this belief, ROAD has been involved in community organisation/empowerment process and programmes with special emphasis on women. ROAD has been forming women's Sanghas in villages. It provides guidance and training to them to take up several programmes including issues affecting their own lives and their community which are hitherto the domains of men in the rural scenario.

ROAD's decision to work with women is not because it is more easy to work with them but it is because they are able to participate well in the programmes. It is surmised that women are the basis and nucleus of development, and that they are more susceptible to changes. Quite often, they tend to serve larger interests with their collective wisdom.

STRATEGIES BEFORE ELECTIONS

ROAD organised several training programmes, some of which were on awareness, motivation, leadership and Panchayat Raj. In cases where women were afraid of contesting, especially from Dalit communities and washermen community (Appendix 11.1), more encouragement and guidance were given.

Firstly, the organisation sent some of the staff members for Panchayat Raj training programmes with Legal Resources for Social Action (LRSA) and VRDP, in addition to their own in-house training programmes conducted on their own and together with South Indian Producers' Association (SIPA). The literature was madc available to the staff to prepare themselves to train the villagers. Similarly, video cassettes of AREDS and Action Aid were brought and used as resource materials.

To begin with, ROAD provided information on Panchayat elections and the possibilities of using PRIs as a vehicle to implement various development programmes in their own villages. ROAD also initiated discussions on how the members of the Sangham could discuss and select consensus candidates from among themselves, the procedures that need to be followed while filing nominations, the methods of campaigning, the ethics they need to follow, taking advantage of reservation for women. The rules and regulations that will govern the elected persons, the roles and responsibilities that they should shoulder, etc., were discussed. ROAD also organised Panchayat Raj Training to the representatives of the Sangham, viz., Chairperson, Secretary, Treasurer, Village Level Animators and some women with potential to contest in the election. ROAD has also considered several options to intensively participate in Panchayat Raj elections. Resource constraints were also discussed. A question on whether one should spend any money towards the campaign expenses of the very poor to contest was also raised. It was resolved not to spend any money for the campaign but to widen the knowledge base and understanding of PRIs in training programmes.

In order to make the members aware of the PRI, a cultural team was formed by ROAD, which developed several street plays, skits, awareness songs and dialogues. A four page pamphlet in vernacular language was also prepared. The cultural team continuously journeyed through 54 villages in the project area for 15 days, moving from one village to another. The local Sangham organised food and accommodation wherever possible and also helped to organise the cultural programmes.

During the day time, the cultural team distributed the pamphlets to adults and explained about PRI. It also explained the involvement of Sangham people and candidates in the development of villages in the past and promises were made that the candidates would continue to commit for the public causes. The cultural programmes mainly focused on the following:

* Structure of three-tier Panchayat Raj system.
* Roles and responsibilities.
* Reservations for the oppressed Dalits and women.
* Voter's rights and duties.
* Effective participation of women and women Sangha members in the election processes.
* Campaigning for candidates from Sanghas.

DURING THE ELECTION

Potential candidates were identified in the Sangha. Special preparatory meetings with the potential candidates and interested women were called for and more intensive training was given. Voter's list was obtained. When threats and intimidation surfaced, women candidates were encouraged not to withdraw. Wherever it was felt essential, ROAD staff went along with the candidates for canvassing.

Totally, 15 candidates were fielded during the Panchayat Raj elections, more or less on the decisions of the Sangha. Out of them, 12 got elected as Ward members. One of the ex-ROAD part-timer (a man), got elected as Panchayat president. Among the three are Dalits, six belong to the most backward classes, one belong to Dhobi (washerman) community and the rest belong to backward classes.

AFTER THE ELECTION

Common meetings were organised to congratulate the elected members. Elected members were cautioned as to their increased responsibilities and duties towards the society. ROAD has made plans to organise a series of training and follow-up programmes for: (i) all the Ward members; (ii) all the Panchayat presidents; (iii) all the Panchayat council members; (iv) all the Sangha women to act as watch dog committees; (v) the villagers; and (vi) the organisation is also planning to organise common functions to introduce all the elected members to the public and also for everyone to know that ROAD is planning to establish PRI resource centre at Shoolagiri and provide training, etc. Discussions have also been initiated with women federation members about forming 'Labour Contract Societies' in the Blocks.

FUTURE ACTION

ROAD has planned to take-up the following programmes in the future:

Orientation: The elected members are unaware of the new Panchayat system, proceedings and amendments. Unless educated properly, the system may not function effectively. Hence, ROAD has planned to organise orientation programmes for all the PRI elected members in its project area.

Rapport with the Sangha: As the women Sanghas are conscious of development activities of their own villages, the Sanghas should have good rapport with the local PRI elected members. Hence, steps are being taken to establish good rapport between these local organisations. For which, Sangha members need training, so also the elected representatives and general public.

Educating the public: In the new PRI, the Gram Sabha plays a major role. The Gram Sabha members in all the Panchayats need to be trained on their rights and duties.

Watch-dog system: Most of the developmental programmes are being channelised through village Panchayat. They would need monitoring to avoid poor quality of work and material pilferage, particularly in civil engineering works. Hence, the Sanghas are being trained and motivated to become watch-dogs of all the government and other programmes.

CONCLUSION

Now the task ahead is to help the elected representatives and the others perform for the well-being of the villages. Many of the elected members do not seem to know the present system of PRI and it is, therefore, essential to organise intensive and systematic training programmes and exposures for all the concerned. If democracy has to succeed with its real meaning, if women have to perform and really get empowered on sustainable basis, a constructive role is to be played by various actors, people, elected representatives, Sanghas, NGOs, donors and government.

APPENDIX 11.1: CASE STUDY OF A VILLAGE PRI MEMBER

Neelammal, aged 35, is a washerwoman. She got elected as a Ward member from Karubala village of Peddasigaralapalli Panchayat, Hosur Taluk. The Panchayat consists of 9 ward members, of which Karubala Ward member seat was allotted for women (general).

Neelammal is a poor landless married woman and is one of the active members of the village Sangha. The village Sangha was formed in 1995 with 24 women members belonging to backward castes. When Neelammal and others approached for enrolling themselves in the Sangha, other members refused to accept her because of her caste. ROAD made continuous and serious attempts to convince the members and this resulted in accepting other caste women into the Sangha. However, eight BC women members strongly objected and wanted to dissolve the Sangha if Dalits had to join. When this was not permitted, they left the Sangha. Only then Neelammal joined. She motivated other members of the village, including four Dalit women, to join the Sangha.

Neelammal played a major role in the strengthening of the Sangha. She regularly attended the training programmes on leadership, awareness motivation programmes, team building and other programmes organised by the ROAD and actively participated. She got exposed to watershed programmes, income generation activities, etc., by visiting other NGOs. Because of her active participation, she is regarded highly by Sangha members and she was elected as a Secretary of the village Sangha.

When the schedule for the Panchayat Raj elections was announced, the Sangha members proposed her to contest as a Ward member. But the high castes disliked her and planned to nominate a candidate from their own community. Since they had no dynamic woman like Neelammal, they dropped the plan to contest in the election. Later, she was elected unanimously from her Ward as a member. The village elders and high castes could not tolerate her selection and were waiting to take revenge on her.

One day, when Neelammal went to fetch water from the public water tap, she had a quarrel with a Muslim woman regarding priority in taking water from the tap. This led to pushing each other and pulling each other's hair. In this process, the Muslim lady sustained minor injury.

Though this was a minor incident, the villagers twisted it as a communal issue since there existed animosity between BCs and Muslims. They egged the Muslim woman to lodge a complaint against Neelammal in the police station. ROAD staff met the local police and requested them not to take further action on the complaint for some time. Subsequently, they discussed with the Muslim woman and convinced her to withdraw the case.

The village traditional Panchayat, consisting of village elders, is headed by a person who does not like ROAD's activities, and obstructs the development works in several ways. Since Neelammal got elected as a Ward member with the support of ROAD, he wanted to take revenge of Neelammal. So, the traditional Panchayat members discussed the issue and fined her Rs. 1,500 which is the highest in the area for such a petty matter. Though Neelammal's relatives requested the Panchayat members to reduce the fine, they refused and warned her that if she does not pay the fine within three days, she will not be allowed to take water from any pipe or well in the village. Fearing disturbances to the functioning of the Sangha by men, the women Sangha was not prepared to take up the issue. The Sangha, of course, helped to pay the fine amount by giving her a loan from the Sangha fund.

Now, Neelammal wonders whether she should continue as Ward member or not? If she continues, she is not sure that similar sufferings will not come to her. But Sangha members are encouraging her to continue without losing courage.

NOTES ON CONTRIBUTORS

Abdul Aziz is Professor of Economics and Project Director, Decentralized Governance and Planning at the Institute for Social and Economic Change, Bangalore. Prior to joining the Institute, Professor Aziz worked at the Shri Ram Centre for Industrial Relations and Human Resources, New Delhi, and taught Economics at Mysore University. Besides directing several research projects, he has published 24 books and numerous research papers in professional journals.

Narinder Bedi graduated in Science and completed Masters in Chemical Engineering from the University of California, USA. He is presently working as a social activist and is Head of Young India Project, Penukonda, Andhra Pradesh, which is working in six districts of Andhra Pradesh. He is the author of three books and has written several articles on rural development.

M.K. Bhat is the Director of Development Support Initiative, based at Bangalore, and Principal Consultant for South India to NOVIB. After participation in mass movements in Karnataka for one and a half decades, he is now focusing his work on NGOs, social activism and development, with a perspective of sustainable development and empowerment of the poor.

Susanne Dam Hansen is Project Officer, UNDP, Tanzania. Prior to this assignment, she was research scholar at the International Development Studies, Roskilde University Centre, Denmark, where she did research on how different development actors at the village level approach to integrate women in natural resource management in Burkina Faso, Africa.

K. Murugesan is the Project Coordinator for the organization SHARE, Vellore, Tamil Nadu. He founded SHARE in 1991, and enabled a large number of women to obtain income through the production of palm-leaf products. Mr. Murugesan has over 20 years of experience in rural development.

D. Rajasekhar is a development economist based at the Institute for Social and Economic Change, Bangalore. He has published seven books and numerous articles in Indian and international journals on rural credit, NGO savings and credit programmes, interface between decentralised government and NGOs, interface between government and NGOs, agrarian change and transformation, irrigation and rural development.

K. Sivaji is the Secretary of Sanghamitra Service Society, Vijayawada, Andhra Pradesh. After working for 15 years in rural development, he gained experience in Community Development Projects at University of Sussex, London, and in fund raising programmes of B.F.W., Germany. Thrice awarded by A.P. State Government for the Rural Development Services, he is the Executive Committee Member of District Literacy Committee, Environment Committee, Prohibition Committee, and a State Resource Person for Micro Planning Programmes of Andhra Pradesh.

G. Suvarchala has been studying the dynamic relationship between political mobilisation and participation through institution building and distribution of developmental benefits at grassroots level. As a consultant for several international funding agencies, she interacted with many NGOs to observe this phenomenon during the last half-a-decade.

Alex Tuscano is Director of PRAXIS, a rural development NGO, working in Bangalore Rural District in Karnataka. He has been involved in development work for the last 15 years.

Mohammed Usman is the Director of a rural development NGO called ROAD, Dharmapuri, Tamil Nadu. He earlier worked as Programme Officer in Oxfam.

Neil Webster is a Senior Research Fellow at the Centre for Development Research, Copenhagen, Denmark, specialising in research into local institutions and rural development in India. He has written extensively on the politics of agrarian development in the states of West Bengal and Karnataka with a particular focus on PRIs and local NGOs.

Index